MEDITERRANEAN DIE COOKBOOK FOR BEGINNERS

1200 DAYS OF EASY-TO-MAKE & TASTY RECIPES WITH A 30 DAYS MEAL PLAN TO KICKSTART YOUR NEW HEALTHY LIFESTYLE AND RE-START ENJOYING LIFE.

Poula Ray

Table of Contents

1. Introduction

The Mediterranean diet has grown in popularity in recent years, and it's simple to understand why: it provides an incredibly broad range of health advantages, starting from cardiovascular health to cancer prevention and exercises motivation.

Beyond its scientifically-proven benefits of health, the Mediterranean diet is widely regarded as one of the best diets since it accommodates diet preferences, promotes flavor and food diversity, and includes items from all groups of food, removing the restricted feelings associated with many diets.

Every diet, of course, has drawbacks, but the Mediterranean diet may bring long-term behavioral improvements and a shift of lifestyle, both of them which actually are important for long-term health. Here's a breakdown of all of the health advantages of eating a Mediterranean-style diet.

Lower your Chance of the Heart Diseases

If the Mediterranean diet is famous for anything, it is for being heart-healthy. As a result, it is consistently ranked as one of the top diets in the Best Diet category by the U.S.A News and the World Report.

It's easy to see why: a slew of scientific evidence suggests that a Mediterranean diet is excellent for the heart.

Everyone who eats the Mediterranean diet is considered a lower probability to acquire heart disease, according to a 2016 study of over 20,000 adults, and the group of researchers believes that roughly 4% of around all the cardiovascular disease cases may be averted if people adopted the Mediterranean diet.

Another study examined the chance of heart attacks, strokes, and cardiovascular disease mortality in persons who ate the Mediterranean diet vs. those who didn't. The five-year study discovered that persons who ate a Mediterranean diet had a 30% decreased risk of heart disease.

Weight Loss Assistance

The Mediterranean diet is a good way to lose weight. A Mediterranean diet actually has been found in studies to aid with losing fat. Mediterranean diet followers lose fat at a similar pace to low-carb followers. A big study released in 2018 found that eating a Mediterranean diet lowers the risk of abdominal obesity (with over 32,000 participants).

Reduces the Chance of Having the stroke

Researchers have found that a Mediterranean diet can prevent up to around 6% of cases of heart disease in the same study that suggested a Mediterranean diet can prevent up to around 8.5% of strokes.

In addition, the 2018 study from the United Kingdom discovered that eating a Mediterranean diet decreased the chance of stroke.

Despite the fact that the study's authors point out that this result only applies to women and that further research is required, they do state that more research is necessary.

Patients with Arthritis May Benefit from the Mediterranean Diet

According to limited data, the Mediterranean diet may assist persons with arthritis in lessening pain. A Mediterranean diet includes several anti-inflammatory foods, which makes sense considering that arthritis is an inflammatory disorder.

In addition, the (NIH) National Institute of Health advises omega-three fatty acids to reduce inflammation, and a Mediterranean diet provides a variety of these beneficial fats.

Possibility of Lowering LDL Cholesterol and Blood Pressure

LDL cholesterol and blood pressure (sometimes known as "negative" cholesterol) are 2 of the most important health and disease risk markers. Any extremely large marker may indicate or be a health issue in and of itself.

The Mediterranean diet, for example, is one of the various ways for regulating and decreasing blood pressure and cholesterol LDL.

Individualized Dietary Requirements Are Possible

The Mediterranean diet will keep you alive whether you're a vegan, paleo, vegetarian, dairy-free, gluten-free, or anything else. Obviously, the diet is most effective when every one of the foods it encourages is permitted, but you actually can tailor it to your unique needs.

Most experts consider the Mediterranean diet to be non-restrictive because it has a fair balance of carbohydrates, healthy fats, proteins, vegetables, fruits, and even a few treats (calling out all the lovers of red wine!).

Physical Activity is Encouraged

One of the fewer diets that promote physical activities as a foundation of a healthy lifestyle is the Mediterranean diet. Most individuals in the country of United States do not get enough exercise, so this is a welcome improvement.

Daily exercises are also much more probably to create healthy eating choices during the day.

It's worth noting, however, that the Mediterranean diet and exercise may be mutually beneficial: Researchers discovered that eating a Mediterranean diet rather than a standard Western diet can actually increase physical performance in a comparable study.

Chapter 1:   Breakfast Recipes

Recipe 1: Artichoke Frittata

Serving Size: 4

Cooking Time: 10 minutes

Ingredients:

- 8 large eggs
- ¼ cup of Asiago cheese, grated
- 1 tablespoon of fresh basil, chopped
- 1 teaspoon of fresh oregano, chopped
- Pinch of salt
- 1 teaspoon of extra virgin olive oil
- 1 teaspoon of garlic, minced
- 1 cup of canned artichokes, drained
- 1 tomato, chopped

Directions:

1. Pre-heat your oven to broil. Take a medium bowl and whisk eggs, Asiago cheese, oregano, basil, sea salt, and pepper.
2. Blend in a bowl. In a large ovenproof skillet, heat the olive oil. Sauté for 1 minute after adding the garlic. Take the skillet from the heat and add the egg mixture. Return skillet to heat and sprinkle artichoke hearts and tomato over eggs.
3. Cook frittata without stirring for 8 minutes. Broil skillet for 1 minute until lightly browned. Cut frittata into 4 pieces and serve. Enjoy!

Nutritional Value: Calories 199; Fat 13g; Carbohydrates 5g; Protein 16g

Recipe 2: Avocado Baked Eggs

Serving Size: 2

Cooking Time: 25 minutes

Ingredients:

- 2 eggs
- 1 medium sized avocado, halved and pit removed
- ¼ cup cheddar cheese, shredded
- Kosher salt and black pepper, to taste

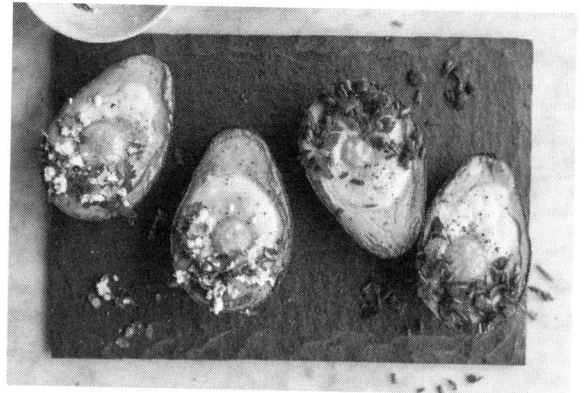

Directions:

1. Preheat oven to a heat of 425 degrees and grease a muffin pan.
2. Crack open an egg into each half of the avocado and season with salt and black pepper.
3. Top with cheddar cheese and transfer the muffin pan in the oven.
4. Bake for about 15 minutes and dish out to serve.

Nutritional Value: Calories 210; Fat 16.6g; Carbohydrates 6.4g; Protein 10.7g

Recipe 3: Bacon and Brie Omelet Wedges

Serving Size: 6

Cooking Time: 10 minutes

Ingredients:

- 2 tablespoons olive oil
- 7 ounces smoked bacon
- 6 beaten eggs
- Small bunch chives, snipped
- 3 ½ ounces brie, sliced
- 1 teaspoon red wine vinegar
- 1 teaspoon Dijon mustard
- 1 cucumber, halved, deseeded, and sliced diagonally
- 7 ounces radish, quartered

Directions:

1. Dissolve In a large saucepan over medium heat, melt 2 tablespoons of butter. Mix in the thyme and halibut and cook
2. Uncover and put it back into the oven for another 20 minutes until it's bubbling. Let it rest for 15 minutes. You can sprinkle it with some parsley before serving.

Nutritional Value: Calories 343; Fat 15.4g; Carbohydrates 39.4g; Protein 13.8g

Recipe 4: Baked Pasta

Serving Size: 8

Cooking Time: 40 minutes

Ingredients:

- 14.1 oz of short pasta
- 21.1 oz of tomato pulp
- 5.3 oz diced ham
- 10.5 oz of mozzarella cheese
- 5.3 oz of grated Parmesan cheese
- 1.7 oz of cleaned onion
- 1.7 oz clean celery
- 1.7 oz clean carrots
- 2.1 oz Extra Virgin Olive Oil
- 1 clove of garlic
- 2 pinches of pepper
- 2 teaspoons salt
- 2 cups water

Directions:

1. In a kitchen mixer, chop the mozzarella cheese with the pepper and Parmesan cheese. Keep aside. Chop the onion, celery and carrot.
2. Heat the prepared oil in a large pot and sauté the chopped celery, carrot and onion for 5 minutes.
3. Add the tomato pulp and salt to the pot and cook for 10 minutes.
4. Preheat the oven to 482°F.
5. Add 2 cups of prepared water to the tomato and then the pasta. Bake for 10 minutes.
6. When done, transfer to an ovenproof dish, add half of the cheese mixture and diced prosciutto and mix well.
7. Sprinkle with the other half of the cheese mixture and bake for 10 minutes.
8. Remove from oven and serve.

Nutritional Value: Calories 217; Fat 28.2g; Carbohydrates 52.5g; Protein 26g

Recipe 5: Buttery Pancakes

Serving Size: 5

Cooking Time: 10 minutes

Ingredients:

- 1 cup wheat flour, whole-grain
- 1 teaspoon baking powder
- 1 teaspoon lemon juice
- 3 eggs, beaten
- ¼ cup Splenda
- 1 teaspoon vanilla extract
- 1/3 cup blueberries
- 1 tablespoon olive oil
- 1 teaspoon butter
- 1/3 cup milk

Directions:

1. In the mixer bowl, combine together baking powder, wheat flour, lemon juice, eggs, Splenda, vanilla extract, milk, and olive oil.
2. Blend the liquid until it is smooth and homogenous.
3. After this, toss the butter in the skillet and melt it.
4. With the help of the ladle pour the pancake batter in the hot skillet and flatten it in the shape of the pancake.
5. Sprinkle the pancake with the blueberries gently and cook for 1.5 minutes over the medium heat.
6. Then flip the pancake onto another side and cook it for 30 seconds more.
7. Repeat the same steps with all remaining batter and blueberries.
8. Transfer the cooked pancakes in the serving plate.

Nutritional Value: Calories 152; Fat 7.5g; Carbohydrates 30.6g; Protein 7.4g

Recipe 6: Carrot and Bran Mini Muffins

Serving Size: 18

Cooking Time: 18 minutes

Ingredients:

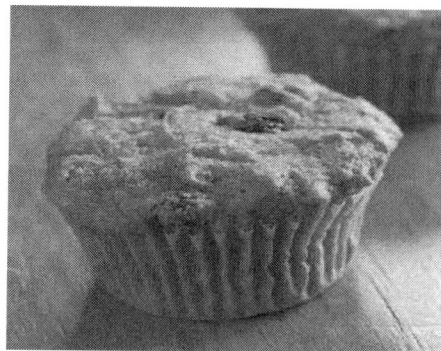

- Nonstick cooking spray
- 1 cup oat bran
- 1 cup whole-wheat flour
- 1/2 cup all-purpose flour
- 1/2 cup old-fashioned oats
- 3 tablespoons packed brown sugar
- 1 teaspoon baking soda
- 1 teaspoon baking powder
- 2 teaspoons ground cinnamon
- 2 teaspoons ground ginger
- 1/2 teaspoon ground nutmeg
- 1/4 teaspoon sea salt
- 11/4 cups unsweetened almond milk
- 2 tablespoons honey
- 1 egg
- 2 tablespoons extra-virgin olive oil
- 11/2 cups grated carrots
- 1/4 cup raisins

Directions:

1. Preheat the oven to 350°F.
2. Coat with nonstick cooking spray.
3. Whisk the oat bran, whole-wheat and all-purpose flours, oats, brown sugar, baking soda, baking powder, cinnamon, ginger, nutmeg, and salt in a large bowl. Set aside.
4. Whip the almond milk, honey, egg, and olive oil.
5. Merge all ingredients and fold until just blended. The batter will be lumpy, with streaks of flour remaining.
6. Fold in the carrots and raisins.
7. Fill each muffin cup three-fourths full.
8. Cool on a wire rack before serving.

Nutritional Value: Calories 115; Fat 3g; Carbohydrates 20g; Protein 2g

Recipe 7: Cheesy Eggs in Avocado

Serving Size: 2

Cooking Time: 15 minutes

Ingredients:

- 1 medium avocado
- 2 organic eggs
- ¼ cup shredded cheddar cheese
- Salt and freshly cracked black pepper
- 1 tablespoon olive oil

Directions:

1. Switch on the oven, then set its temperature to 425°F, and let preheat.
2. Meanwhile, prepare the avocados and for this, cut the avocado in half and remove its pit.
3. Take two muffin tins, grease them with oil, and then add an avocado half into each tin.
4. Crack an egg into each avocado half, season well with salt and freshly cracked black pepper, and then sprinkle cheese on top.
5. When the oven has preheated, place the muffin tins in the oven and bake for 15 minutes until cooked.
6. When done, take out the muffin tins, transfer the avocados baked organic eggs to a dish, and then serve them.

Nutritional Value: Calories 210; Fat 16.6g; Carbohydrates 6.4g; Protein 10.7g

Recipe 8: Cheesy Green Bites

Serving Size: 8

Cooking Time: 15 minutes

Ingredients:

- ¼ cup frozen chopped kale
- ¼ cup finely chopped artichoke hearts
- ¼ cup ricotta cheese
- 2 tablespoons grated Parmesan cheese
- ¼ cup Goat cheese
- 1 large egg white
- 1 teaspoon dried basil
- 1 lemon, zested
- ½ teaspoon salt
- ½ teaspoon freshly ground black pepper
- 4 frozen filo dough, thawed
- 1 tablespoon extra-virgin olive oil

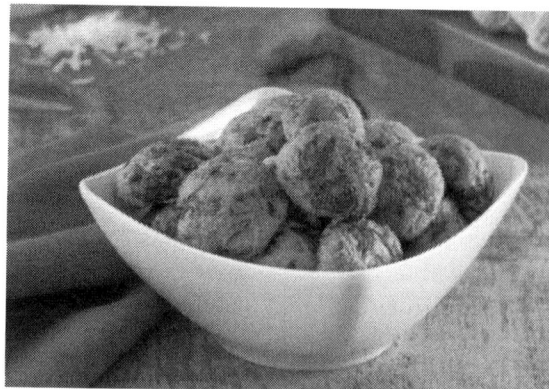

Directions:

1. Combine kale, artichoke, ricotta, Parmesan, Goat cheese, egg white, basil, lemon zest, salt, and pepper in a bowl. Place a filo dough on a clean flat surface. Brush with olive oil.
2. Place a second filo sheet on the first and brush with more oil. Continue layering to form a pile of four oiled sheets. Working from the short side, cut the phyllo sheets into 8 strips and half them.
3. Spoon 1 tablespoon of filling onto one short end of every strip. Fold a corner to cover the filling and a triangle; continue folding over and over to the end of the strip, creating a triangle-shaped filo packet.
4. Repeat the process with the other filo bites. Place a trivet into the pot. Pour in 1 cup of water. Place the bites on top of the trivet. Cook on High Pressure for 15 minutes after sealing the lid. Do a quick release.

Nutritional Value: Calories 326; Fat 25g; Carbohydrates 38g; Protein 13.3g

Recipe 9: Creamy Parsley Soufflé

Serving Size: 2

Cooking Time: 25 minutes

Ingredients:

- 2 fresh red chili peppers, chopped
- Salt, to taste
- 4 eggs
- 4 tablespoons light cream
- 2 tablespoons fresh parsley, chopped

Directions:

1. Preheat the oven to a heat of 375 degrees F and grease 2 soufflé dishes.
2. Combine all the ingredients in a bowl and mix well.
3. Put the mixture into prepared soufflé dishes and transfer in the oven.
4. Cook for about 6 minutes and dish out to serve immediately.
5. For meal prepping, you can refrigerate this creamy parsley soufflé in the ramekins covered in a foil for about 2-3 days.

Nutritional Value: Calories 108; Fat 9g; Carbohydrates 1.1g; Protein 6g

Recipe 10: Egg White Scramble with Cherry Tomatoes and Spinach

Serving Size: 4

Cooking Time: 10 minutes

Ingredients:

- 1 tablespoon Olive oil
- 1 whole Egg
- 10 Egg whites
- ¼ teaspoon Black pepper
- ½ teaspoon Salt
- 1 garlic clove, minced
- 2 cups cherry tomatoes, halved
- 2 cups packed fresh baby spinach
- ½ cup Light cream or Half & Half
- ¼ cup finely grated parmesan cheese

Directions:

1. Whisk the eggs, pepper, salt, and milk. Prepare a skillet using the med-high temperature setting. Toss in the garlic when the pan is hot to sauté for approximately 30 seconds.
2. Pour in the tomatoes and spinach and continue to sauté it for one additional minute. The spinach should be wilted, and the tomatoes softened.
3. Add the egg mixture into the pan using the medium heat setting. Fold the egg gently as it cooks for about two to three minutes. Remove from the burner, and sprinkle with a sprinkle of cheese.

Nutritional Value: Calories 142; Fat 2g; Carbohydrates 4g; Protein 15g

Recipe 11: Fig and Ricotta Overnight Oats

Serving Size: 1

Cooking Time: 0 minutes

Ingredients:

- 2 tablespoons chopped dried figs
- 1 tablespoon toasted sliced almonds
- ½ cup rolled oats
- 2 teaspoons honey, sweetener
- ¼ teaspoon salt
- 2 tablespoons shredded ricotta cheese
- ½ cup water

Directions:

1. Take a large bowl, add oats, salt, and water, and stir until well mixed.
2. Cover the bowl with its lid, place it into the refrigerator and let it rest overnight.
3. Then, uncover the bowl, spoon the prepared oatmeal into a serving bowl, and sprinkle almonds, figs, and ricotta cheese on top.
4. Then, drizzle honey on top, and serve.

Nutritional Value: Calories 295; Fat 8.5g; Carbohydrates 47.5g; Protein 10.4g

Recipe 12: Greek Breakfast Bagel

Serving Size: 2

Cooking Time: 5 minutes

Ingredients:

- ½ cup baby spinach
- 1 tablespoon crumbled feta cheese
- 1 Plain Bagel
- 1 teaspoon olive oil
- 8 cherry tomatoes, halved
- 2 eggs
- Freshly ground pepper
- Pinch each salt

Directions:

1. Beat the eggs, spice, and peppers together; set them aside.
2. Heat the olive oil over medium-high heat in a frying pan; fry the vegetables for about four minutes, or begin to soften.
3. Insert spinach; fry for around two minutes until it is wilted moderately.
4. Put in beaten egg; fry for three or four minutes or until soft curds begin to develop from the egg mixture.
5. Mix in cheese from the feta. Spoon over the halves of bagels.

Nutritional Value: Calories 125; Fat 1g; Carbohydrates 40g; Protein 4g

Recipe 13: Heavenly Egg Bake with Blackberry

Serving Size: 4

Cooking Time: 15 minutes

Ingredients:

- Chopped rosemary
- 1 teaspoon lime zest
- ½ teaspoon salt
- ¼ teaspoon vanilla extract, unsweetened
- 1 teaspoon grated ginger
- 3 tablespoon coconut flour
- 1 tablespoon unsalted butter
- 5 organic eggs
- 1 tablespoon olive oil
- ½ cup fresh blackberries
- Black pepper to taste

Directions:

2. Switch on the oven, then set its temperature to 350°F and let it preheat.
3. Meanwhile, place all the ingredients in a blender, reserving the berries and pulse for 2 to 3 minutes until well blended and smooth.
4. Take four silicon muffin cups, grease them with oil, evenly distribute the blended batter in the cups, top with black pepper and bake for 15 minutes until cooked through and the top has golden brown.
5. When done, let blueberry egg bake cool in the muffin cups for 5 minutes, then take them out, cool them on a wire rack and then serve.
6. For meal prepping, wrap each egg bake with aluminum foil and freeze for up to 3 days.
7. When ready to eat, reheat blueberry egg bake in the microwave and then serve.

Nutritional Value: Calories 144; Fat 10g; Carbohydrates 2g; Protein 8.5g

Recipe 14: Hummus Deviled Egg

Serving Size: 6

Cooking Time: 10 minutes

Ingredients:

- 1/4 cup of finely diced cucumber
- 1/4 cup of finely diced tomato
- 2 teaspoons of fresh lemon juice
- 1/8 teaspoon salt
- 6 hard-cooked peeled eggs, sliced half lengthwise
- 1/3 cup of roasted garlic hummus or any hummus flavor
- Chopped fresh parsley (optional)

Directions:

1. Combine the tomato, lemon juice, cucumber, and salt together, and then gently mix. Scrape out the yolks from the halved eggs and store them for later use.
2. Scoop a heaping teaspoon of hummus in each half egg. Top with parsley and half-teaspoon tomato-cucumber mixture. Serve immediately.

Nutritional Value: Calories 90; Fat 2g; Carbohydrates 9g; Protein 4g

Recipe 15: Lean and Green Chicken Pesto Pasta

Serving Size: 1

Cooking Time: 15 minutes

Ingredients:

- 3 cups raw kale leaves
- 2 tablespoon olive oil
- 2 cups fresh basil
- 1/4 teaspoon salt
- 3 tablespoon lemon juice
- 3 garlic cloves
- 2 cups cooked chicken breast
- 1 cup baby spinach
- 6 oz. uncooked chicken pasta
- 3 oz. diced fresh mozzarella
- Basil leaves or red pepper flakes to garnish

Directions:

1. Start by making the pesto, add the kale, lemon juice, basil, garlic cloves, olive oil, and add salt to a blender and blend until smooth.
2. Add pepper to taste.
3. Cook the pasta and strain off the water. Reserve 1/4 cup of the liquid.
4. Get a bowl and mix everything, the cooked pasta, pesto, diced chicken, spinach, mozzarella, and the reserved pasta liquid.
5. Sprinkle the mixture with additional chopped basil or red paper flakes (optional).
6. Now your salad is ready. You may serve it warm or chilled. Also, it can be taken as a salad mix-ins or as a side dish. Leftovers should be stored in the refrigerator inside an air-tight container for 3–5 days.

Nutritional Value: Calories 244; Fat 10g; Carbohydrates 22.5g; Protein 20.5g

Recipe 16: Mediterranean Frittata

Serving Size: 6

Cooking Time: 30 minutes

Ingredients:

- 9 eggs
- ¼ cup olive oil
- ½ cup chopped onions
- 1 medium zucchini cut into ½-inch cubes
- 4oz/113g crumbled feta cheese
- 1/3 cup freshly grated parmesan cheese
- 8 chopped pitted kalamata olives
- 1 diced sweet red pepper
- ½ teaspoon pepper
- ½ teaspoon salt
- 1/3 cup of thinly sliced fresh basil leaves

Directions:

1. Preheat the oven to 220°C/425°F.
2. In a large skillet greased with 1 to 2 tablespoon of olive oil, sauté the Kalamata olives, zucchini, red pepper, and onion over medium-high heat till tender.
3. Whisk the eggs with the feta cheese, fresh basil, salt, and pepper, then combine it with the sautéed vegetables and cover to cook for 10 to 12 minutes.
4. Remove from heat and sprinkle with parmesan and extra virgin olive oil.
5. Broil 5 ½-inch from the heat with the oven door partially open for 2- minutes.
6. Serve the frittata warm, cut into wedges.

Nutritional Value: Calories 288; Fat 7.7g; Carbohydrates 5.6g; Protein 15.3g

Recipe 17: Mediterranean Omelet

Serving Size: 2

Cooking Time: 12 minutes

Ingredients:

- 2 teaspoons extra-virgin olive oil
- 1 garlic clove
- 1/2 red bell pepper
- 1/2 yellow bell pepper
- 1/4 cup thinly sliced red onion
- 2 tablespoons chopped fresh basil
- 2 tablespoons chopped fresh parsley
- 1/2 teaspoon salt
- 1/2 teaspoon black pepper
- 4 large eggs, beaten

Directions:

1. In a big heavy pan, heat 1 teaspoon olive oil. Sauté the garlic, peppers, and onion in the pan for 5 minutes, stirring occasionally.
2. Cook for 2 minutes with the basil, parsley, salt, and pepper. Return the pan to heat after removing the vegetable mixture to a dish.
3. Pour the beaten eggs into the hot 1 teaspoon olive oil, stirring to coat evenly. 3–5 minutes, or until the rims are boiling and the eggs are dry except for the middle.
4. To turn the omelet over, either flip it or use a spatula.
5. Spoon the vegetable mixture over one-half of the omelet and fold the empty side over the top with a spatula. Place the omelet on a cutting board or a plate.
6. Cut the omelet in half and top with fresh parsley to serve.

Nutritional Value: Calories 197; Fat 18g; Carbohydrates 41g; Protein 6g

Recipe 18: Mushroom and Zucchini Egg Muffins

Serving Size: 4

Cooking Time: 20 minutes

Ingredients:

- 2 tablespoons of olive oil
- 1 cup of Parmesan, grated
- 1 onion, chopped
- 1 cup of mushrooms, sliced
- 1 red bell pepper, chopped
- 1 zucchini, chopped
- Salt and black pepper to taste
- 8 eggs, whisked
- 2 tablespoons of chives, chopped

Directions:

1. Preheat the oven to 360 F. Warm the olive oil in a skillet over medium heat and sauté onion, bell pepper, zucchini, mushrooms, salt, and pepper for 5 minutes until tender.
2. Mix with the whisked eggs and season with salt and pepper. Distribute the mixture across muffin cups and top with the Parmesan cheese. Sprinkle with chives and bake for 10 minutes. Serve.

Nutritional Value: Calories 160; Fat 4g; Carbohydrates 4g; Protein 5g

Recipe 19: Nectarin Bruschetta

Serving Size: 2

Cooking Time: 15 minutes

Ingredients:

- 1 ½ tablespoon of white wine vinegar
- 1 teaspoon of honey
- 1 nectarine, sliced
- ¼ cup of olive oil
- 2 teaspoons of black pepper
- ⅓ cup of fresh ricotta cheese
- 2 slices of bread, toasted

Directions:

1. Mix the teaspoon of honey and the tablespoon of white wine vinegar in a medium-sized bowl. Stir in the sliced nectarine, mix it well and marinate for approximately about 10 minutes.
2. Add the black pepper and olive oil, then mix well. Spread the cup of fresh ricotta cheese over the slices of toasted bread. Divide the nectarine and its juice on top of the bread. Serve.

Nutritional Value: Calories 247; Fat 29.1g; Carbohydrates 18.5g; Protein 6.4g

Recipe 20: Parmesan Ham Frittata

Serving Size: 2

Cooking Time: 15 minutes

Ingredients:

- 1/4 cup chopped onion
- 1/4 cup chopped green pepper
- 2 garlic cloves, minced
- 2 tablespoons olive oil
- 4 eggs
- Salt and pepper to taste
- 1/2 cup cubed fully cooked ham
- 1/4 cup grated Parmesan cheese

Directions:

1. In the 6-inch broiler-proof skillet, sauté garlic, green pepper, and onion in oil. Lower the heat to the medium: whip pepper, salt, and eggs in a bowl. Pour ham and egg mixture into vegetables.
2. When eggs are set, lift the edges, allowing the uncooked portion to flow under. Once eggs become almost set, drizzle with cheese. Broil for 1 to 2 minutes, 4 to 5 inches away from the heat source, until the eggs are set.

Nutritional Value: Calories 151; Fat 6.6g; Carbohydrates 6.4g; Protein 16.4g

Recipe 21: Poached Eggs with Avocado Puree

Serving Size: 4

Cooking Time: 5 minutes

Ingredients:

- 2 avocados, peeled and pitted
- 1/4 cup chopped fresh basil leaves
- 3 tablespoons red wine vinegar
- Juice of 1 lemon
- Zest of 1 lemon
- 1 garlic clove, minced
- 1 teaspoon sea salt
- 1/8 teaspoon freshly ground black pepper
- Pinch cayenne pepper, plus more as needed
- 4 eggs

Directions:

1. Combine the avocados, basil, 2 tablespoons vinegar, lemon juice and zest, garlic, 1/2 teaspoon salt, pepper, and cayenne in a blender. Purée for 1 minute, or until completely smooth.
2. Pour approximately three-quarters of a cup of water into a 12-inch nonstick pan and set it over medium heat. Add the remaining 1/2 teaspoon sea salt and 1/4 cup vinegar. Bring the water to a low boil, then reduce to low heat.
3. Crack the eggs carefully into the custard cups. Carefully slide the eggs into the simmering water, one at a time, while holding the cups slightly above the water. Wait 5 minutes without stirring or raising the lid.
4. Carefully take the eggs from the water and allow them to drain completely. Place each egg on a dish and drizzle with the avocado purée.

Nutritional Value: Calories 213; Fat 20g; Carbohydrates 11g; Protein 2g

Recipe 22: Quinoa Muffins

Serving Size: 12

Cooking Time: 30 minutes

Ingredients:

- 1 cup quinoa, cooked
- 6 eggs, whisked
- Salt and black pepper to the taste
- 1 cup Swiss cheese, grated
- 1 small yellow onion, chopped
- 1 cup white mushrooms, sliced
- ½ cup sun-dried tomatoes, chopped

Directions:

1. In a bowl, combine the eggs with salt, pepper and the rest of the ingredients and whisk well.
2. Divide this into a silicone muffin pan, bake at 350°F for 30 minutes and serve for breakfast.

Nutritional Value: Calories 123; Fat 5.6g; Carbohydrates 10.8g; Protein 7.5g

Recipe 23: Raspberry Oats

Serving Size: 1

Cooking Time: 15 minutes

Ingredients:

- ½ cup of fresh raspberries
- ¼ teaspoon of vanilla
- ¾ cup of unsweetened almond milk
- 1 teaspoon of honey
- 2 teaspoon of chia seeds
- ⅓ cup of rolled oats
- Pinch of salt

Directions:

1. Add raspberries into the bowl and mash using the fork. Transfer mash raspberries and remaining ingredients into the glass jar and stir everything well.
2. Cover the glass jar with lid and place in refrigerator for overnight. Add little drizzle of milk and serve. Add one to two drops of almond extracts.

Nutritional Value: Calories 189; Fat 11.1g; Carbohydrates 41.8g; Protein 8.5g

Recipe 24: Rice Stuffed Tomatoes

Serving Size: 5

Cooking Time: 1 hour and 20 minutes

Ingredients:

- ¼ - ½ cup tomato pulp
- 2-3 tablespoons olive oil
- 6 sprigs of Italian parsley
- 1 clove garlic chopped
- 4-5 tomatoes
- 1 teaspoon basil
- ½ teaspoon salt
- 1 teaspoon oregano
- 1 cup (185 grams) uncooked rice

Directions:

1. Before preheating the oven to 375°, heat oil in a big basin. Rice in water for 1 hour, then rinsed and drained. Wash and chop a tomato to lay aside. Separate the veggies' pulp and seeds.
2. In a medium dish, combine tomato paste, oregano, cinnamon, parsley, cloves, olive oil, and rice.
3. Cover tomato mixture. Replace the tomato tops, add salt, and glaze with olive oil. Cook the potatoes and rice for 45-50 minutes with the rosemary. Ready-to-eat.

Nutritional Value: Calories 151; Fat 6.6g; Carbohydrates 6.4g; Protein 16.4g

Recipe 25: Spinach Artichoke Egg Casserole

Serving Size: 2

Cooking Time: 45 minutes

Ingredients:

- 1/8 cup milk
- 2.5-ounce frozen chopped spinach, thawed and drained well
- 1/8 cup parmesan cheese
- 1/8 cup onions, shaved
- ¼ teaspoon salt
- ¼ teaspoon crushed red pepper
- 4 large eggs
- 3.5-ounce artichoke hearts, drained
- ¼ cup white cheddar, shredded
- 1/8 cup ricotta cheese
- ½ garlic clove, minced
- ¼ teaspoon dried thyme

Directions:

1. Preheat the oven to a heat of 350 degrees F and grease a baking dish with non-stick cooking spray.
2. Whisk eggs and milk together and add artichoke hearts and spinach.
3. Mix well and stir in rest of the ingredients, withholding the ricotta cheese.
4. Pour the mixture into the baking dish and top evenly with ricotta cheese.
5. Transfer in the prepared preheated oven and bake for about 30 minutes.
6. Dish out and serve warm.

Nutritional Value: Calories 228; Fat 13.3g; Carbohydrates 10.1g; Protein 19.1g

Recipe 26: Stuffed Pita Breads

Serving Size: 4

Cooking Time: 15 minutes

Ingredients:

- 1 and ½ tablespoons olive oil
- 1 tomato, cubed
- 1 garlic clove, minced
- 1 red onion, chopped
- ¼ cup parsley, chopped
- 15 ounces canned fava beans, drained and rinsed
- ¼ cup lemon juice
- Salt and black pepper to the taste
- 4 whole-wheat pita bread pockets

Directions:

1. In a medium-hot pan, heat the oil and sauté the onion for 5 minutes.
2. Stir in the other ingredients and simmer for another 10 minutes.
3. Serve the pita pockets stuffed with this mixture for breakfast.

Nutritional Value: Calories 382; Fat 1.8g; Carbohydrates 66g; Protein 28.5g

Recipe 27: Sun-Dried Tomatoes, Dill and Feta Omelet Casserole

Serving Size: 6

Cooking Time: 40 minutes

Ingredients:

- 1 teaspoon dried oregano
- 12 large eggs
- 1 tablespoon of chopped dill
- 2 cups whole milk
- 8 oz fresh spinach
- 2 cloves garlic, minced
- 12 ounces of artichoke salad with olives and peppers, drained and chopped
- 5 oz sun-dried tomato feta cheese
- 1 teaspoon lemon pepper
- 1 teaspoon salt
- 4 teaspoon olive oil, divided

Directions:

1. Preheat oven to 375 degrees F. Chops the fresh herbs and artichoke salad. In a skillet over medium heat, add 1 tablespoon of olive oil.
2. Sauté the spinach and garlic until wilted, about 3 minutes. Oil a 9x13 inch baking dish, layer the spinach and artichoke salad evenly in the dish
3. Whisk together the eggs, milk, herbs, salt, and lemon pepper in a medium bowl. To serve, pour the egg mixture over the vegetables and sprinkle with feta cheese.
4. Bake for 35-40 minutes in the middle of the oven or until the center is firm to the touch. Allow to cool, slice a and distribute among the storage containers. Store for 2-3 days or freeze for 3 months

Nutritional Value: Calories 196; Fat 12g; Carbohydrates 5g; Protein 10g

Recipe 28: Tomato and Spinach Egg Wraps

Serving Size: 2

Cooking Time: 15 minutes

Ingredients:

- 1 tablespoon of parsley, chopped
- 1 tablespoon of olive oil
- ¼ onion, chopped
- 3 sun-dried tomatoes, chopped
- 3 large eggs, beaten
- 2 cups of baby spinach, torn
- 1 ounces of feta cheese, crumbled
- Salt to taste
- 2 whole-wheat tortillas, warm

Directions:

1. Warm the olive oil in a large-sized pan over medium heat. Sauté the onion and tomatoes for about 3 minutes. Add the prepared beaten eggs and stir to scramble them, about 4 minutes.
2. Add the spinach and parsley stir to combine. Sprinkle the feta cheese over the eggs. Season with salt to taste. Divide the mixture between the tortillas. Roll them up and serve.

Nutritional Value: Calories 435; Fat 28g; Carbohydrates 31g; Protein 17g

Recipe 29: Tuna Breakfast Quiche

Serving Size: 4

Cooking Time: 30 minutes

Ingredients:

- 3 eggs
- 3 tablespoons of oats
- 3 tablespoons of cream cheese
- 1 tablespoon of dill
- 1 tablespoon of basil
- 1 cup of can tuna, drained
- ½ onion, chopped
- ½ carrot, grated
- ½ zucchini, grated
- Salt and pepper

Directions:

1. Preheat the oven to 350° F. In a bowl, whisk eggs with cream cheese, pepper, and salt. Add remaining ingredients and stir until well combined.
2. Pour egg mixture into the greased quiche pan and bake in preheated oven for 20 minutes. Allow to cool then slice and serve.

Nutritional Value: Calories 151; Fat 6.6g; Carbohydrates 6.4g; Protein 16.4g

Recipe 30: Zucchini Oats

Serving Size: 4

Cooking Time: 10 minutes

Ingredients:

- 2 cups rolled oats
- 2 cups of water
- ½ teaspoon salt
- 1 tablespoon butter
- 1 zucchini, grated
- ¼ teaspoon ground ginger

Directions:

1. Pour water in the saucepan.
2. Add rolled oats, butter, and salt.
3. Stir gently and start to cook the oats for 4 minutes over the high heat.
4. When the mixture starts to boil, add ground ginger and grated zucchini. Stir well.
5. Cook the oats for 5 minutes more over the medium-low heat.

Nutritional Value: Calories 189; Fat 5.7g; Carbohydrates 29.4g; Protein 6g

Recipe 31: Artichoke Beef Roast

Serving Size: 6

Cooking Time: 45 minutes

Ingredients:

- 2 lbs beef roast, cubed
- 1 tablespoon garlic, minced
- 1 onion, chopped
- 1/2 teaspoon paprika
- 1 tablespoon parsley, chopped
- 2 tomatoes, chopped
- 1 tablespoon capers, chopped
- 10 oz can artichokes, drained and chopped
- 2 cups chicken stock
- 1 tablespoon olive oil
- Pepper
- Salt

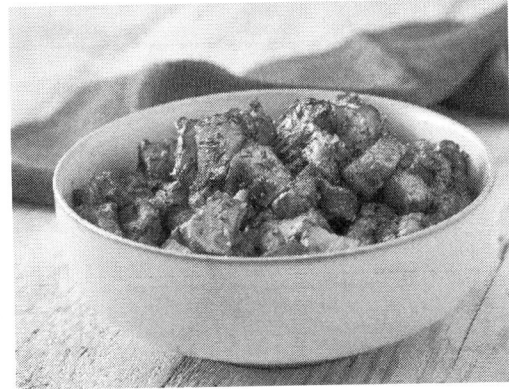

Directions:

1. Add oil into the prepared instant pot and set the pot on sauté mode.
2. Add garlic and onion and sauté for 5 minutes.
3. Add meat and cook until brown.
4. Add remaining ingredients and stir well.
5. Seal pot with cover lid and cook on high for 35 minutes.
6. Once done, allow to release pressure naturally. Remove lid.
7. Serve and enjoy.

Nutritional Value: Calories 344; Fat 12.2g; Carbohydrates 9.2g; Protein 48.4g

Recipe 32: Asparagus Risotto

Serving Size: 4

Cooking Time: 30 minutes

Ingredients:

- 5 cups vegetable broth
- 3 tablespoons unsalted butter
- 1 tablespoon olive oil
- 1 small onion, chopped
- 1½ cups Arborio rice
- 1-pound fresh asparagus
- ¼ cup of Parmesan cheese, grated, plus more for serving

Directions:

1. Bring the vegetable broth to a boil in a medium saucepan. Reduce to low heat and maintain the broth at a constant simmer.
2. In a 4-quart heavy-bottomed saucepan over medium heat, melt 2 tablespoons of butter with the olive oil. Add the onion and cook for 2 to 3 minutes.
3. Stir in the rice with a wooden spoon for 1 minute, or until the grains are well coated in the butter and oil.
4. Stir in ½ cup of warm broth. Cook, often stirring, for about 5 minutes until the broth is completely absorbed.
5. Add the asparagus stalks and another ½ cup of broth. Cook, often stirring until the liquid is absorbed. Continue adding the broth, ½ cup at a time, and cooking until it is completely absorbed before adding the next ½ cup. Stir frequently to prevent sticking. The rice should be cooked yet firm after approximately 20 minutes.
6. Add the asparagus tips, the remaining 1 tablespoon of butter, and the Parmesan cheese. Stir vigorously to combine.
7. Remove from the heat, top with additional Parmesan cheese, if desired, and serve immediately.

Nutritional Value: Calories 434; Fat 14g; Carbohydrates 13g; Protein 10g

Recipe 33: Baked Salmon with Garlic Cilantro Sauce

Serving Size: 6

Cooking Time: 15 minutes

Ingredients:

- 2 pounds salmon fillet, skinless, frozen, thawed
- 1 large tomato, sliced into rounds
- 5 teaspoons chopped garlic
- 1 cup stems trimmed cilantro, fresh
- ½ large lime, sliced into rounds
- ¼ teaspoon ground black pepper
- ¼ teaspoon salt, divided
- ½ cup olive oil
- 3 tablespoons lime juice

Directions:

1. Switch on the prepared preheated oven, set the temperature to 425 degrees F, or 218 degrees C, and let it preheat.
2. Meanwhile, take a large baking pan, spray it with cooking spray to grease it, and then set it aside until required.
3. Plugin a food processor, add garlic, cilantro, salt, oil, lime juice, and pulse until well mixed.
4. Then transfer the prepared cilantro and garlic sauce into a small bowl, and set it aside until required.
5. Place the salmon fillet onto the prepared baking pan, and sprinkle salt and black pepper all around to season it.
6. Then spoon the prepared sauce on top of the salmon, spread it evenly until coated, and place the tomato slices, and lime slices on top.
7. Place the baking pan on the second shelf of the oven, and bake for 5 minutes, or until almost done.
8. Then, cover the baking pan with aluminum foil, and bake for another 7 minutes, or until cooked.
9. When done, place the prepared salmon on a serving plate, and serve immediately.

Nutritional Value: Calories 302; Fat 16.7g; Carbohydrates 5.4g; Protein 34.4g

Recipe 34: Broiled Salmon

Serving Size: 4

Cooking Time: 20 minutes

Ingredients:

- 4 (3oz/85g) fillet salmon
- 1 tablespoon chopped fresh cilantro
- 4 pressed garlic cloves
- ½ cup olive oil
- ¼ cup balsamic vinegar
- 1 ½ teaspoon garlic salt
- 1 tablespoon chopped fresh basil

Directions:

1. A little bowl with olive oil and balsamic vinegar. Grease a baking dish and place the salmon on it. Rub garlic on the salmon fillets, then pour the vinegar-oil mixture over them, turning once to coat. Season with salt, basil, and cilantro. Set aside to marinate for 10 minutes
2. Preheat the oven's broiler to 450°F/230°C.
3. Place the salmon approximately 6 inches from the heat source and let it boil for 15 minutes, or until it is browned on both sides and flakes easily with your fingers. Brush with sauce from the pan.

Nutritional Value: Calories 390; Fat 5.4g; Carbohydrates 3.6g; Protein 15g

Recipe 35: Carrot Mushroom Beef Roast

Serving Size: 4

Cooking Time: 40 minutes

Ingredients:

- 1 1/2 lbs beef roast
- 1 teaspoon paprika
- 1/4 teaspoon dried rosemary
- 1 teaspoon garlic, minced
- 1/2 lb mushrooms, sliced
- 1/2 cup chicken stock
- 2 carrots, sliced
- Pepper
- Salt

Directions:

1. Add all prepared ingredients into the inner pot of instant pot and stir well.
2. Seal pot with cover lid and cook on high for 40 minutes.
3. Once done, allow to eventually release pressure naturally for 10 minutes then release remaining using quick release. Remove lid.
4. Slice and serve.

Nutritional Value: Calories 345; Fat 10.9g; Carbohydrates 5.6g; Protein 53.8g

Recipe 36: Cayenne Cod and Tomatoes

Serving Size: 4

Cooking Time: 25 minutes

Ingredients:

- 1 teaspoon lime juice
- Salt and black pepper to the taste
- 1 teaspoon sweet paprika
- 1 teaspoon cayenne pepper
- 2 tablespoons olive oil
- 1 yellow onion, chopped
- 2 garlic cloves, minced
- 4 cod fillets, boneless
- A pinch of cloves, ground
- ½ cup chicken stock
- ½ pound cherry tomatoes, cubed

Directions:

1. Heat up a pan with the oil over medium-high heat add the cod, salt, pepper and the cayenne, cook for 4 minutes on each side and divide between plates.
2. Heat up the same pan over medium-high heat, add the onion and garlic and sauté for 5 minutes.
3. Add the rest of the ingredients, stir, bring to a simmer and cook for 10 minutes more.
4. Divide the mix next to the fish and serve.

Nutritional Value: Calories 232; Fat 16.5g; Carbohydrates 24.8g; Protein 16.5g

Recipe 37: Chicken and Mint Sauce

Serving Size: 4

Cooking Time: 30 minutes

Ingredients:

- 2 and ½ tablespoons olive oil
- 2 pounds chicken breasts, skinless, boneless and halved
- 3 tablespoons garlic, minced
- 2 tablespoons lemon juice
- 1 tablespoon red wine vinegar
- 1/3 cup Greek yogurt
- 2 tablespoons mint, chopped
- A pinch of salt and black pepper

Directions:

1. In a blender, combine the garlic with the lemon juice and the other ingredients except the oil and the chicken and pulse well.
2. Heat up a pan with the oil over medium-high heat, add the chicken and brown for 3 minutes on each side.
3. Add the mint sauce, introduce in the oven and bake everything at 370 degrees F for 25 minutes.
4. Divide the mix between plates and serve.

Nutritional Value: Calories 278; Fat 12g; Carbohydrates 18.1g; Protein 13.3g

Recipe 38: Chicken Kebabs

Serving Size: 4

Cooking Time: 20 minutes

Ingredients:

- 2 chicken breasts, skinless, boneless, and cubed
- 1 red bell pepper, cut into squares
- 1 red onion, roughly cut into squares
- 2 teaspoons sweet paprika
- 1 teaspoon nutmeg, ground
- 1 teaspoon Italian seasoning
- ¼ teaspoon smoked paprika
- A pinch of salt and black pepper
- ¼ teaspoon cardamom, ground
- Juice of 1 lemon
- 3 garlic cloves, minced
- ½ cup olive oil

Directions:

1. Combine the chicken with the onion, the bell pepper, and the other ingredients, toss well, cover the bowl and keep in the fridge for 30 minutes.
2. Assemble skewers with chicken, peppers, and onions, place them on your preheated grill and cook over medium heat for 8 minutes on each side.
3. Divide the kebabs between plates and serve with a side salad.

Nutritional Value: Calories 262; Fat 14g; Carbohydrates 14g; Protein 20g

Recipe 39: Dijon Fish Fillets

Serving Size: 2

Cooking Time: 5 minutes

Ingredients:

- 2 white fish fillets
- 1 tablespoon Dijon mustard
- 1 cup of water
- Pepper
- Salt

Directions:

1. Pour water into the prepared instant pot and place trivet in the pot.
2. Brush fish fillets with mustard and season with pepper and salt and place on top of the trivet.
3. Seal pot with lid and cook on high for 3 minutes.
4. Once done, release pressure using quick release. Remove lid.
5. Serve and enjoy.

Nutritional Value: Calories 270; Fat 11.9g; Carbohydrates 0.5g; Protein 38g

Recipe 40: Grilled Lemon Chicken

Serving Size: 4

Cooking Time: 20 minutes

Ingredients:

- 24oz/680g skinless, boneless chicken breast halves
- ½ cup fresh lemon juice
- ½ cup soy sauce
- ½ teaspoon ground ginger
- ¼ teaspoon ground black pepper

Directions:

1. Rinse and wipe dry the chicken breasts with paper towels after removing them from the refrigerator. In a bowl, stir the lemon juice, ginger, soy sauce, and black pepper, then pour it into a resealable plastic bag. Add the chicken breast into the bag and sell. Massage to coat the chicken with lemon juice. Refrigerate the marinated chicken for at least 20 minutes and up to 24 hours.
2. Preheat the oven to 400°F/204°C. Lightly grease a grill grate and place about 4 inches from the heat source.
3. Retrieve the chicken breasts from the marinade and prepare a grill. Sauté chicken for 6–8 minutes each side or until cooked through.

Nutritional Value: Calories 214; Fat 4.1g; Carbohydrates 5.3g; Protein 37.6g

Recipe 41: Herb and Pistachio Turkey Breasts

Serving Size: 4

Cooking Time: 50 minutes

Ingredients:

- ½ cup of pistachios, toasted and chopped
- 1 tablespoon of olive oil
- 1 pound of turkey breast, cubed
- 1 cup of chicken stock
- 1 tablespoon of basil, chopped
- 1 tablespoon of rosemary, chopped
- 1 tablespoon of oregano, chopped
- 1 tablespoon of parsley, chopped
- 1 tablespoon of tarragon, chopped
- 3 garlic cloves, minced
- 3 cups of tomatoes, chopped

Directions:

1. Warm the olive oil in a large-sized skillet over medium heat and cook turkey and garlic for 5 minutes.
2. Stir in stock, basil, rosemary, oregano, parsley, tarragon, pistachios, and tomatoes and bring to a simmer. Cook for 35 minutes. Serve immediately.

Nutritional Value: Calories 310; Fat 12g; Carbohydrates 20g; Protein 25g

Recipe 42: Herbed Almond Turkey

Serving Size: 4

Cooking Time: 40 minutes

Ingredients:

- 1 big turkey breast, skinless, boneless and cubed
- 1 tablespoon olive oil
- ½ cup chicken stock
- 1 tablespoon basil, chopped
- 1 tablespoon rosemary, chopped
- 1 tablespoon oregano, chopped
- 1 tablespoon parsley, chopped
- 3 garlic cloves, minced
- ½ cup almonds, toasted and chopped
- 3 cups tomatoes, chopped

Directions:

1. Heat up a pan with the oil over medium-high heat, add the turkey and the garlic and brown for 5 minutes.
2. Add the stock and the rest of the ingredients, bring to a simmer over medium heat and cook for 35 minutes.
3. Divide the mix between plates and serve.

Nutritional Value: Calories 297; Fat 11.2g; Carbohydrates 19.4g; Protein 23.6g

Recipe 43: Lamb and Potatoes Stew

Serving Size: 4

Cooking Time: 1 hour and 20 minutes

Ingredients:

- 2 pounds lamb shoulder, boneless and cubed
- Salt and black pepper to the taste
- 1 yellow onion, chopped
- 3 tablespoons olive oil
- 3 tomatoes, grated
- 2 cups chicken stock
- 2 and ½ pounds gold potatoes, cubed
- ¾ cup green olives, pitted and sliced
- 1 tablespoon of cilantro, chopped

Directions:

1. Heat a pot with the oil over medium-high heat, add the lamb, and brown for 5 minutes on each side.
2. Continue to sauté for another 5 minutes after adding the onion.
3. Add the rest of the ingredients, bring to a simmer, cook over medium heat, and cook for 1 hour and 10 minutes.
4. Divide the stew into bowls and serve.

Nutritional Value: Calories 411; Fat 17.4g; Carbohydrates 25.5g; Protein 34.3g

Recipe 44: Mushroom Cream Turkey

Serving Size: 6

Cooking Time: 25 minutes

Ingredients:

- 1 (7-ounce) can peas, drained
- 2 cloves garlic
- 4 tablespoons extra-virgin olive oil
- 1 small onion, chopped
- 1 can mushrooms with juice, sliced
- 1½ pounds turkey breasts, sliced thin
- 2 tablespoons butter
- 3½ ounces half and half cream
- 2 tablespoons tomato sauce
- Salt and ground black pepper to taste
- All-purpose flour as needed

Directions:

1. In a large-sized saucepan or skillet over medium heat, heat 1 tablespoon of the olive oil. Add the onion and stir-cook until soft and translucent. Add the peas and 1 tablespoon of hot water; simmer for 5 minutes. Set aside.
2. In another skillet or saucepan, cook the garlic in 1 tablespoon of the olive oil until aromatic. Mix in the mushrooms with juice and simmer for 9–10 minutes. Set aside.
3. In a bowl, coat the turkey slices in the flour. In another skillet, sauté the turkey until evenly brown in the remaining 2 tablespoons of olive oil.
4. Mix in the cream, tomato sauce, cooked peas and mushrooms. Simmer until the sauce becomes smooth and pink. Add salt and pepper to taste. Serve warm.

Nutritional Value: Calories 233; Fat 14.7g; Carbohydrates 1.8g; Protein 23.3g

Recipe 45: Oyster Stew

Serving Size: 6

Cooking Time: 1 hour and 10 minutes

Ingredients:

- 2 garlic cloves, minced
- ¼ cup jarred roasted red peppers
- 2 teaspoons oregano, chopped
- 1-pound lamb meat, ground
- 1 tablespoon red wine vinegar
- Salt and black pepper to the taste
- 1 teaspoon red pepper flakes
- 2 tablespoons olive oil
- 1 and ½ cups chicken stock
- 36 oysters, shucked
- 1 and ½ cups canned black-eyed peas, drained

Directions:

1. Heat the oil in a saucepan over medium heat, add the meat and garlic and cook for 5 minutes.
2. Add the peppers and the rest of the ingredients, bring to a simmer and cook for 15 minutes.
3. Divide the stew into bowls and serve.

Nutritional Value: Calories 264; Fat 9.3g; Carbohydrates 2.3g; Protein 1.2g

Recipe 46: Pan-Seared Trout with Tzatziki

Serving Size: 4

Cooking Time: 20 minutes

Ingredients:

- 1 cucumber, grated and squeezed
- 3 tablespoons of olive oil
- 4 trout fillets, boneless
- ½ lime, juiced
- Salt and black pepper to taste
- 1 garlic clove, minced
- 1 teaspoon of sweet paprika
- 4 garlic cloves, minced
- 2 cups of Greek yogurt
- 1 tablespoon of dill, chopped

Directions:

1. Warm the prepared 2 tablespoons of the olive oil in a skillet over medium heat. Sprinkle the trout with salt, pepper, lime juice, garlic, and paprika and sear for 8 minutes on all sides. Remove to a paper towel–lined plate.
2. Combine cucumber, garlic, remaining olive oil, yogurt, salt, and dill in a bowl. Share trout into plates and serve with tzatziki.

Nutritional Value: Calories 400; Fat 19g; Carbohydrates 19g; Protein 41g

Recipe 47: Pesto Fish Fillet

Serving Size: 4

Cooking Time: 10 minutes

Ingredients:

- 4 halibut fillets
- 1/2 cup water
- 1 tablespoon lemon zest, grated
- 1 tablespoon capers
- 1/2 cup basil, chopped
- 1 tablespoon garlic, chopped
- 1 avocado, peeled and chopped
- Pepper
- Salt

Directions:

1. Add lemon zest, capers, basil, garlic, avocado, pepper, and salt into the blender blend until smooth.
2. Place fish fillets on aluminum foil and spread a blended mixture on fish fillets.
3. Fold foil around the fish fillets.
4. Pour water into the prepared instant pot and place trivet in the pot.
5. Place foil fish packet on the trivet.
6. Seal pot with lid and cook on high for 8 minutes.
7. Once done, allow to release pressure naturally. Remove lid.
8. Serve and enjoy.

Nutritional Value: Calories 426; Fat 16.6g; Carbohydrates 5.5g; Protein 61.8g

Recipe 48: Sage Tomato Beef

Serving Size: 4

Cooking Time: 40 minutes

Ingredients:

- 2 lbs beef stew meat, cubed
- 1/4 cup tomato paste
- 1 teaspoon garlic, minced
- 2 cups chicken stock
- 1 onion, chopped
- 2 tablespoon olive oil
- 1 tablespoon sage, chopped
- Pepper
- Salt

Directions:

1. Add oil into the prepared instant pot and set the pot on sauté mode.
2. Add garlic and onion and sauté for 5 minutes.
3. Add meat and sauté for 5 minutes.
4. Add remaining ingredients and stir well.
5. Seal pot with cover lid and cook on high for 30 minutes.
6. Once done, allow to release pressure naturally. Remove lid.
7. Serve and enjoy.

Nutritional Value: Calories 515; Fat 21.5g; Carbohydrates 7g; Protein 70g

Recipe 49: Sailor Clams

Serving Size: 2

Cooking Time: 30 minutes

Ingredients:

- 2 lbs. fresh cherrystone clams
- 3 tablespoons olive oil
- 1 tablespoon minced garlic
- 1/2 onion, minced
- 1/2 cup dry white wine
- 1 pinch saffron threads
- 1 teaspoon crushed red pepper flakes
- 1/4 teaspoon vegetable bouillon powder
- salt to taste
- 1 tablespoon all-purpose flour
- 1/2 cup water
- 1 teaspoon chopped fresh parsley

Directions:

1. Put clams in a saucepan with a tight-fitting cover then pour in enough water to cover the clams. Secure the lid then boil the clams on high heat. Let it steam for 3-5 minutes until the clams open. Drain and keep the clam water.
2. On medium heat, heat oil in a large-sized pan. Add onion and garlic and cook and stir for 3 minutes until the onion is see through and soft. Add the prepared white wine and turn heat to high. Put in vegetable bouillon, red pepper flakes, and saffron to season. Pour in the reserved clam water and boil.
3. Combine water and flour until dissolved. Pour into the sauce and mix until thick If required, add salt to taste. Put in the clams in their shells and mix until they are covered with sauce. Serve with chopped parsley on top.

Nutritional Value: Calories 347; Fat 21.7g; Carbohydrates 12.5g; Protein 14.8g

Recipe 50: Salmon and Creamy Endives

Serving Size: 4

Cooking Time: 15 minutes

Ingredients:

- 4 salmon fillets, boneless
- 2 endives, shredded
- Juice of 1 lime
- Salt and black pepper to the taste
- ¼ cup chicken stock
- 1 cup Greek yogurt
- ¼ cup green olives pitted and chopped
- ¼ cup fresh chives, chopped
- 3 tablespoons olive oil

Directions:

1. Heat up a pan with half of the oil over medium heat, add the endives and the rest of the ingredients except the chives and the salmon, toss, cook for 6 minutes and divide between plates.
2. Heat up another pan with the rest of the oil, add the salmon, season with salt and pepper, cook for 4 minutes on each side, add next to the creamy endives mix, sprinkle the chives on top and serve.

Nutritional Value: Calories 266; Fat 13.9g; Carbohydrates 23.8g; Protein 17.5g

Recipe 51: Scallions and Salmon Tartar

Serving Size: 4

Cooking Time: 0 minutes

Ingredients:

- 4 tablespoons scallions, chopped
- 2 teaspoons lemon juice
- 1 tablespoon chives, minced
- 1 tablespoon olive oil
- 1 pound salmon, skinless, boneless and minced
- Salt and black pepper to the taste
- 1 tablespoon parsley, chopped

Directions:

1. In a bowl, combine the scallions with the salmon and the rest of the ingredients, stir well, divide into small moulds between plates and serve.

Nutritional Value: Calories 224; Fat 14.5g; Carbohydrates 12.7g; Protein 5.3g

Recipe 52: Seafood Gumbo

Serving Size: 4

Cooking Time: 30 minutes

Ingredients:

- ¼ cup tapioca flour
- ¼ cup olive oil
- 1 cup celery, chopped
- 1 white onion, chopped
- 1 red bell pepper, chopped
- 1 green bell pepper, chopped
- 1 red chili, chopped
- 2 cups okra, chopped
- 2 garlic cloves, minced
- 1 cup canned tomatoes, crushed
- 1 teaspoon thyme, dried
- 2 cups fish stock
- 1 bay leaf
- 16 ounces canned crab meat, drained
- 1-pound shrimp, peeled and deveined
- ¼ cup parsley, chopped
- Salt and black pepper to the taste

Directions:

1. Heat a pot with the oil over medium heat, add the flour, whisk to obtain a paste, and cook for about 5 minutes.
2. Add the bell peppers, the onions, celery, and the okra and sauté for 5 minutes.
3. Stir in the other ingredients (except the crab, shrimp, and parsley), reduce to low heat, and cook for 15 minutes.
4. Add the remaining ingredients, simmer the soup for 10 minutes more, divide into bowls and serve.

Nutritional Value: Calories 363; Fat 2g; Carbohydrates 18g; Protein 40g

Recipe 53: Shrimp Lunch Rolls

Serving Size: 4

Cooking Time: 0 minutes

Ingredients:

- 12 rice paper sheets, soaked in warm water and drained
- 1 cup of cilantro, chopped
- 12 basil leaves
- 12 baby lettuce leaves
- 1 small cucumber, sliced
- 1 cup of carrots, shredded
- 20 ounces of shrimp, cooked, peeled, and deveined

Directions:

1. Arrange all rice papers on a working surface, divide cilantro, bay leaves, baby lettuce leaves, cucumber, carrots, and shrimp, wrap, seal edges, and serve lunch.
2. Enjoy!

Nutritional Value: Calories 200; Fat 4g; Carbohydrates 14g; Protein 8g

Recipe 54: Spiced Chicken Meatballs

Serving Size: 4

Cooking Time: 20 minutes

Ingredients:

- 1 pound chicken meat, ground
- 1 tablespoon pine nuts, toasted and chopped
- 1 egg, whisked
- 2 teaspoons turmeric powder
- 2 garlic cloves, minced
- Salt and black pepper to the taste
- 1 and ¼ cups heavy cream
- 2 tablespoons olive oil
- ¼ cup parsley, chopped
- 1 tablespoon chives, chopped

Directions:

1. In a large-sized bowl, combine the chicken with the pine nuts and the rest of the ingredients except the oil and the cream, stir well and shape medium meatballs out of this mix.
2. Heat up a pan with the oil over medium-high heat, add the meatballs and cook them for 4 minutes on each side.
3. Add the cream, toss gently, cook everything over medium heat for 10 minutes more, divide between plates and serve.

Nutritional Value: Calories 283; Fat 9.2g; Carbohydrates 24.4g; Protein 34.5g

Recipe 55: Swordfish Pizzaiola

Serving Size: 4

Cooking Time: 20 minutes

Ingredients:

- 4 slices of swordfish
- 4.4 oz of Mozzarella
- 14.1 oz of cherry tomatoes
- 1 cloves of garlic
- 1 handful of capers
- 10 black olives
- 1 teaspoon of oregano
- 4 tablespoons of extra virgin olive oil
- salt and pepper one pinch

Directions:

1. Prepare an emulsion by mixing the oil with the minced garlic, oregano, salt and pepper. Place the swordfish slices in a bowl, cover them with the emulsion and let them marinate for 30 minutes.
2. Meanwhile, blanch the cherry tomatoes in a pot of boiling water and slice the mozzarella. Let the tomatoes cool down, peel them and cut them into cubes.
3. After 30 minutes, transfer the swordfish to a baking sheet and cover each slice with the mozzarella slices, tomato cubes, capers and olives. Bake in a preheated at a heat of 356°F oven for 15-20 minutes.
4. Serve the pizzaiola swordfish piping hot.

Nutritional Value: Calories 405; Fat 18.9g; Carbohydrates 5.9g; Protein 48.9g

Recipe 56: Thyme Ginger Garlic Beef

Serving Size: 2

Cooking Time: 45 minutes

Ingredients:

- 1 lb beef roast
- 2 whole cloves
- 1/2 teaspoon ginger, grated
- 1/2 cup beef stock
- 1/2 teaspoon garlic powder
- 1/2 teaspoon thyme
- 1/4 teaspoon pepper
- 1/4 teaspoon salt

Directions:

1. Mix together ginger, cloves, thyme, garlic powder, pepper, and salt and rub over beef.
2. Place meat into the instant pot. Pour stock around the meat.
3. Seal pot with cover lid and cook on high for 45 minutes.
4. Once done, release pressure using quick release. Remove lid.
5. Shred meat using a fork and serve.

Nutritional Value: Calories 452; Fat 15.7g; Carbohydrates 5.2g; Protein 70.1g

Recipe 57: Tomato Olive Fish Fillets

Serving Size: 4

Cooking Time: 10 minutes

Ingredients:

- 2 lbs halibut fish fillets
- 2 oregano sprigs
- 2 rosemary sprigs
- 2 tablespoon fresh lime juice
- 1 cup olives, pitted
- 28 oz can tomatoes, diced
- 1 tablespoon garlic, minced
- 1 onion, chopped
- 2 tablespoon olive oil

Directions:

1. Add oil into the inner pot of instant pot and set the pot on sauté mode.
2. Add onion and sauté for 3 minutes.
3. Add garlic and sauté for a minute.
4. Add lime juice, olives, herb sprigs, and tomatoes and stir well.
5. Seal pot with lid and cook on high for 3 minutes.
6. Once done, release pressure using quick release. Remove lid.
7. Add fish fillets and seal pot again with lid and cook on high for 2 minutes.
8. Once done, release pressure using quick release. Remove lid.
9. Serve and enjoy.

Nutritional Value: Calories 333; Fat 19.1g; Carbohydrates 31.8g; Protein 13.4g

Recipe 58: Trout and Tzatziki Sauce

Serving Size: 4

Cooking Time: 10 minutes

Ingredients:

- Juice of ½ lime
- Salt and black pepper to the taste
- 1 and ½ teaspoon coriander, ground
- 1 teaspoon garlic, minced
- 4 trout fillets, boneless
- 1 teaspoon sweet paprika
- 2 tablespoons avocado oil

For the sauce:
- 1 cucumber, chopped
- 4 garlic cloves, minced
- 1 tablespoon olive oil
- 1 teaspoon white vinegar
- 1 and ½ cups Greek yogurt
- A pinch of salt and white pepper

Directions:

1. Heat up a pan with the avocado oil over medium-high heat, add the fish, salt, pepper, lime juice, 1 teaspoon garlic and the paprika, rub the fish gently and cook for 4 minutes on each side.
2. In a bowl, combine the cucumber with 4 garlic cloves and the rest of the ingredients for the sauce and whisk well.
3. Divide the fish between plates, drizzle the sauce all over and serve with a side salad.

Nutritional Value: Calories 393; Fat 18.5g; Carbohydrates 18.3g; Protein 39.6g

Recipe 59: Veggie Quesadillas

Serving Size: 3

Cooking Time: 4 minutes

Ingredients:

- 1 cup black beans, cooked
- ½ red bell pepper, chopped
- 4 tablespoons cilantro, chopped
- ½ cup corn
- 1 cup low-fat cheddar, shredded
- 6 whole-wheat tortillas
- 1 carrot, shredded
- 1 small jalapeno pepper, chopped
- 1 cup non-fat yogurt
- Juice of ½ lime

Directions:

1. Spread half of the tortillas with the black beans, red bell pepper, 2 tablespoons cilantro, corn, carrot, jalapeño, and cheese, then top with the other half of the tortillas.
2. Preheat a pan with one tortilla. Cook for 3 minutes on one side, flip, and cook for 1 more minute on the other side before transferring to a dish. 3.
3. Repeat the process with the remaining quesadillas.
4. Mix 2 tablespoons of cilantro, yogurt, and lime juice in a small bowl until thoroughly combined. Serve with the quesadillas.
5. Enjoy!

Nutritional Value: Calories 200; Fat 3g; Carbohydrates 13g; Protein 7g

Recipe 60: White Pizza with Broccoli Crust

Serving Size: 2

Cooking Time: 35 minutes

Ingredients:

- 2 1/2 cups broccoli (riced)
- 1 egg
- 1/3 cup + ¾ cup shredded mozzarella cheese (low-fat)
- 1/4 cup grated Parmesan cheese
- 1/2 teaspoon Italian seasoning
- 1/2 cup ricotta cheese (part-skim)
- 1/4 teaspoon red pepper flakes
- 1 garlic clove (minced)
- 1/2 cup broccoli florets (chopped)

Directions:

1. Preheat oven to 400°F.
2. Cook broccoli in a microwave-safe tray and then cover it (about 3 minutes).
3. Once cooled, transfer "rice" to a cheesecloth or clean, thin dishtowel and squeezed out as much liquid as possible.
4. Take a bowl, mix in broccoli, egg, one-third cup Mozzarella cheese, Parmesan cheese, and Italian seasoning, and combine well.
5. Form mixture into a square pizza (1/3 inch thick) onto a baking sheet. Bake until edges are brown (15-20 minutes).
6. Meanwhile, take a bowl, combine ricotta, red pepper flakes, and garlic, and then spread this ricotta mixture onto crust.
7. Bake until cheese is melted (about 5-10 minutes).

Nutritional Value: Calories 279; Fat 16.7g; Carbohydrates 9.5g; Protein 23.8g

Chapter 3: Dinner Recipes

Recipe 61: Baked Falafel

Serving Size: 4

Cooking Time: 10 minutes

Ingredients:

- 2 cups chickpeas, cooked
- 1 yellow onion, diced
- 3 tablespoons olive oil
- 1 cup fresh parsley, chopped
- 1 teaspoon ground cumin
- ½ teaspoon coriander
- 2 garlic cloves, diced

Directions:

1. In the food processor, put all the ingredients and blend until smooth.
2. To 375F, preheat the oven.
3. Then, with the baking paper, cover the baking tray.
4. Create the balls from the mixture of chickpeas and press them gently in the form of the falafel.
5. Place the falafel in the tray and bake for 25 minutes in the oven.

Nutritional Value: Calories 316; Fat 11.2g; Carbohydrates 43.3g; Protein 13.5g

Recipe 62: Baked Oysters with Tasso Cream

Serving Size: 4

Cooking Time: 1 hour and 10 minutes

Ingredients:

- 1/4 cup butter, melted
- 4 slices white bread
- 1/8 teaspoon salt
- 3 ounces Tasso ham, finely chopped
- 1/8 teaspoon pepper
- 2 tablespoon sweet onion, chopped
- 2 cups heavy whipping cream
- 1 garlic clove, minced
- 2 dashes Louisiana-style hot sauce
- 1 dozen fresh shell oysters, scrubbed
- Salt and pepper to taste

Directions:

1. Preheat oven to 300° C.
2. Bake bread for 8-10 minutes on both sides. Make bread crumbs in a processor. Add in salt, melted butter, and pepper. Cook ham until lightly browned over medium heat.
3. Add in garlic and onion. Cook for 1-2 minutes. Add cream. Boil the mixture until half remains. Add salt, hot sauce, and pepper. Heat oven to 350°C. Shuck oysters.
4. Bake oysters sprinkled with bread crumbs for 8-10 minutes. Serve with sauce.

Nutritional Value: Calories 240; Fat 10g; Carbohydrates 17g; Protein 19g

Recipe 63: Cabbage Roll Casserole with Veal

Serving Size: 6

Cooking Time: 4 hours

Ingredients:

- 1-pound raw ground veal
- 1 head of cabbage
- 1 medium green pepper
- 1 medium onion, chopped
- 1 (15-ounce) can of tomatoes
- 2 (15-ounce) cans tomato sauce
- 1 teaspoon minced garlic
- 1 tablespoon Worcestershire sauce
- 1 tablespoon beef bouillon
- ½ teaspoon salt
- ½ teaspoon pepper
- 1 cup uncooked brown rice

Directions:

1. Situate all the ingredients to your slow cooker
2. Stir well to combine.
3. Adjust your slow cooker to high and cook for 4 hours, or cook for 8 hours on low.

Nutritional Value: Calories 335; Fat 18g; Carbohydrates 34g; Protein 22.9g

Recipe 64: Chicken Marsala

Serving Size: 4

Cooking Time: 22 minutes

Ingredients:

- ¼ cup flour
- Salt and pepper to taste
- ¼ teaspoon oregano
- ¼ teaspoon basil
- 4 boneless and skinless chicken breasts pounded very thin.
- ¼ cup butter
- ¼ cup olive oil
- 1 diced onion
- 2 minced garlic cloves
- 1 cup sliced mushrooms
- ¾ cup Marsala wine

Directions:

1. Combine the prepared flour with the herbs, salt and pepper. Dredge the chicken through the seasoned flour.
2. Heat the prepared butter and olive oil in a large skillet and then sauté the garlic and onion for 5 minutes.
3. Add the chicken and mushrooms and brown the chicken on both sides for 5 minutes.
4. Stir in the Marsala and simmer for 12 minutes.

Nutritional Value: Calories 293; Fat 7.3g; Carbohydrates 14.7g; Protein 39.3g

Recipe 65: Chicken Stroganoff

Serving Size: 4

Cooking Time: 20 minutes

Ingredients:

- 1 cup cremini mushrooms, sliced
- 1 onion, sliced
- 1 tablespoon olive oil
- ½ teaspoon thyme
- 1 teaspoon salt
- 1 cup Plain yogurt
- 10 oz chicken fillet, chopped

Directions:

1. Heat up olive oil in the saucepan.
2. Add mushrooms and onion.
3. Sprinkle the vegetables with thyme and salt. Mix up well and cook them for 5 minutes.
4. After this, add chopped chicken fillet and mix up well.
5. Cook the ingredients for 5 minutes more.
6. Then add plain yogurt, mix up well, and close the lid.
7. Cook chicken stroganoff for 10 minutes over the low heat.

Nutritional Value: Calories 224; Fat 9.2g; Carbohydrates 7.4g; Protein 24.2g

Recipe 66: Chicken with Tomato-Balsamic Pan Sauce

Serving Size: 4

Cooking Time: 35 minutes

Ingredients:

- 2 8-ounces boneless chicken breast, skinless
- ½ cup halved, cherry tomatoes
- 2 tablespoons sliced shallot
- 1 tablespoon minced garlic
- ¼ cup white whole-wheat flour
- 1 tablespoon toasted, crushed fennel seeds
- ½ teaspoon ground black pepper, divided
- ½ teaspoon salt, divided
- 3 tablespoons olive oil, divided
- 1 tablespoon softened butter, unsalted
- ¼ cup balsamic vinegar
- 1 cup chicken broth, low-sodium

Directions:

1. Place the prepared chicken on a cutting board and cut the chicken breast horizontally into 4 equal pieces.
2. Cover the chicken pieces with plastic wrap each, and pound the chicken with the smooth side of a mallet until ¼-inch thick.
3. Then, remove the prepared plastic wrap, and sprinkle with salt, and black pepper, to season it on each chicken piece.
4. Take a medium bowl, add flour, coat each piece of chicken with flour, completely shaking off the excess, and then place them on a plate.
5. Take a large skillet pan, place it over medium-high heat, add 2 tablespoons of oil, and when hot, place 2 pieces of chicken and cook each chicken piece for 3 minutes per side or until brown, and well-cooked.
6. When done, place the prepared chicken on a plate and cook the remaining chicken in the same manner.
7. Then add 1 tablespoon of oil into the pan, add tomato, and shallot into it, and cook for 2 minutes, or until soft.
8. Add vinegar, bring the mixture to a boil, cook for 45 seconds, or until the vinegar has reduced by half.
9. Then add broth, garlic, fennel seeds, salt, and black pepper, and cook for 5 minutes, while stirring, until the mixture has reduced by half.
10. Add butter, stir until well mixed, when done, place the prepared chicken on a serving plate, spoon the sauce on the side, and serve.

Nutritional Value: Calories 294; Fat 16.7g; Carbohydrates 9.5g; Protein 25.4g

Recipe 67: Dijon and Herb Pork Tenderloin

Serving Size: 6

Cooking Time: 30 minutes

Ingredients:

- ½ cup fresh Italian parsley leaves
- 3 tablespoons fresh rosemary leaves
- 3 tablespoons fresh thyme leaves
- 3 tablespoons Dijon mustard
- 1 tablespoon extra-virgin olive oil
- 4 garlic cloves, minced
- ½ teaspoon sea salt
- ¼ teaspoon freshly ground black pepper
- 1 (1½-pound) pork tenderloin

Directions:

1. Preheat the oven to 400°F.
2. In a blender, pulse parsley, rosemary, thyme, mustard, olive oil, garlic, sea salt, and pepper. Spread the mixture evenly over the pork and place it on a rimmed baking sheet.
3. Bake for about 20 minutes. Pull out from the oven and put aside for 10 minutes before slicing and serving.

Nutritional Value: Calories 393; Fat 12g; Carbohydrates 74g; Protein 23g

Recipe 68: Eggplant Ratatouille

Serving Size: 2

Cooking Time: 30 minutes

Ingredients:

- 1 eggplant
- 1 sweet yellow pepper
- 3 cherry tomatoes
- 1/3 white onion, chopped
- 1/2 teaspoon of garlic clove, sliced
- 1 teaspoon of olive oil
- 1/2 teaspoon of ground black pepper
- 1/2 teaspoon of Italian seasoning

Directions:

1. Preheat the air fryer to 360 F. Peel the eggplants and chop them. Put the chopped eggplants in the air fryer basket. Place the cherry tomatoes in the air fryer basket. Then add chopped onion, sliced garlic clove, olive oil, ground black pepper, and Italian seasoning.
2. Chop the sweet yellow pepper roughly and add it to the air fryer basket. Shake the vegetables gently and cook for 15 minutes. Stir the meal after 8 minutes of cooking. Transfer the cooked ratatouille to the serving plates. Enjoy!

Nutritional Value: Calories 249; Fat 3.7g; Carbohydrates 28.9g; Protein 5.1g

Recipe 69: Fish Stew with Tomatoes and Olives

Serving Size: 4

Cooking Time: 10 minutes

Ingredients:

- 1 1/2 lb. halibut fillet
- 4 cloves garlic, minced
- 1 cup cherry tomatoes, sliced in half
- 3 cups tomato soup
- 1 cup green olives, pitted and sliced

Directions:

1. Sprinkle salt and pepper over the fish.
2. In the Instant Pot, pour 1 tablespoon olive oil.
3. Cook until the garlic is aromatic.
4. Toss in the fish.
5. Cook for 3 minutes per side.
6. Add the rest of the ingredients.
7. Cover the pot.
8. Select the manual function.
9. Cook at low pressure for 3 minutes.
10. Release the pressure quickly.

Nutritional Value: Calories 245; Fat 3.7g; Carbohydrates 28g; Protein 26.3g

Recipe 70: Garlicky Clams

Serving Size: 4

Cooking Time: 10 minutes

Ingredients:

- 3 lbs clams, clean
- 4 garlic cloves
- 1/4 cup olive oil
- 1/2 cup fresh lemon juice
- 1 cup white wine
- Pepper
- Salt

Directions:

1. Add oil into the inner pot of instant pot and set the pot on sauté mode.
2. Add garlic and sauté for 1 minute.
3. Add wine and cook for 2 minutes.
4. Add remaining ingredients and stir well.
5. Seal pot with lid and cook on high for 2 minutes.
6. Once done, allow to release pressure naturally. Remove lid.
7. Serve and enjoy.

Nutritional Value: Calories 332; Fat 13.5g; Carbohydrates 40.5g; Protein 2.5g

Recipe 71: Greek Lamb Chop

Serving Size: 8

Cooking Time: 8 minutes

Ingredients:

- 8 trimmed lamb loin chops
- 2 tablespoon lemon juice
- 1 tablespoon dried oregano
- 1 tablespoon minced garlic
- ½ teaspoon salt
- ¼ teaspoon black pepper

Directions:

1. Preheat the broiler
2. Combine oregano, garlic, lemon juice, salt, and pepper and rub on both sides of the lamb. Situate lamb on a broiler pan coated with cooking spray and cook for 4 min on each side.

Nutritional Value: Calories 457; Fat 15g; Carbohydrates 49g; Protein 20g

Recipe 72: Ground Pork Skillet

Serving Size: 6

Cooking Time: 25 minutes

Ingredients:

- 2 1/4 pounds ground pork
- 3 tablespoons olive oil
- 1 1/2 bunch kale, trimmed and roughly chopped
- 1 1/2 cup onions, sliced
- 1/3 teaspoon black pepper, or more to taste
- 1/3 cup tomato puree
- 1 1/2 bell pepper, chopped
- 1 1/2 teaspoon sea salt
- 1 1/2 cup chicken bone broth
- 1/3 cup port wine
- 3/4 cloves garlic, pressed
- 1 1/2 chili pepper, sliced

Directions:

1. In a large-sized cast-iron pan over medium-high heat, heat 1 tablespoon of olive oil. Sauté the onion, garlic, and peppers until soft and aromatic; set aside.
2. Cook the ground pork for 5 minutes, or until no longer pink, in the remaining tablespoon of olive oil.
3. Cook for 15 to 17 minutes, or until the other ingredients are cooked thoroughly.
4. Storing
5. The ground pork mixture can be kept in the fridge for up to 3 or 4 days in airtight containers or Ziploc bags.
6. Place the ground pork mixture in airtight containers or heavy-duty freezer bags to freeze. Frozen for up to 3 months Defrost in the refrigerator. Enjoy!

Nutritional Value: Calories 349; Fat 13g; Carbohydrates 4.4g; Protein 45.3g

Recipe 73: Honey Garlic Shrimp

Serving Size: 4

Cooking Time: 10 minutes

Ingredients:

- 1 lb shrimp, peeled and deveined
- 1/4 cup honey
- 1 tablespoon garlic, minced
- 1 tablespoon ginger, minced
- 1 tablespoon olive oil
- 1/4 cup fish stock
- Pepper
- Salt

Directions:

1. Add shrimp into the large bowl. Add remaining ingredients over shrimp and toss well.
2. Transfer shrimp into the instant pot and stir well.
3. Seal pot with lid and cook on high for 5 minutes.
4. Once done, release pressure using quick release. Remove lid.
5. Serve and enjoy.

Nutritional Value: Calories 240; Fat 5.6g; Carbohydrates 20.9g; Protein 26.5g

Recipe 74: Italian Shredded Pork Stew

Serving Size: 8

Cooking Time: 8 hours

Ingredients:

- 2 medium sweet potatoes
- 2 cups fresh kale, chopped
- 1 large onion, chopped
- 4 cloves garlic, minced
- 1 2½–3½ pound boneless pork shoulder butt roast
- 1 (14-ounce) can cannellini beans
- 1½ teaspoons Italian seasoning
- ½ teaspoon salt
- ½ teaspoon pepper
- 3 (14½-ounce) cans chicken broth
- Sour cream (optional)

Directions:

1. Coat slow cooker with nonstick cooking spray or olive oil.
2. Place the cubed sweet potatoes, kale, garlic, and onion into the slow cooker.
3. Add the pork shoulder on top of the potatoes.
4. Add the beans, Italian seasoning, salt, and pepper.
5. Pour the chicken broth over the meat.
6. Cook on low for 8 hours.
7. Serve with sour cream, if desired.

Nutritional Value: Calories 283; Fat 13g; Carbohydrates 24g; Protein 18g

Recipe 75: Jalapeno Beef Chili

Serving Size: 8

Cooking Time: 40 minutes

Ingredients:

- 1 lb ground beef
- 1 teaspoon garlic powder
- 1 jalapeno pepper, chopped
- 1 tablespoon ground cumin
- 1 tablespoon chili powder
- 1 lb ground pork
- 4 tomatillos, chopped
- 1/2 onion, chopped
- 5 oz tomato paste
- Pepper
- Salt

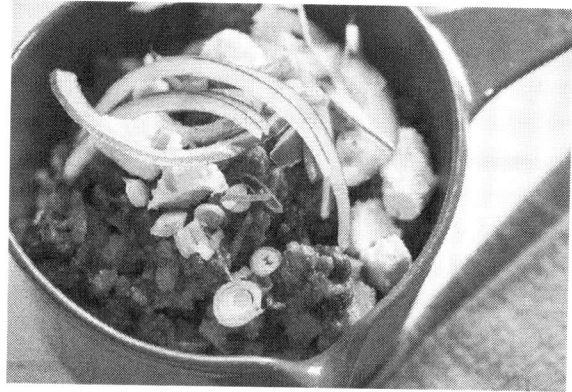

Directions:

1. Add oil into the prepared instant pot and set the pot on sauté mode.
2. Add the prepared beef and pork and cook until brown.
3. Add remaining ingredients and stir well.
4. Seal pot with cover lid and cook on high for 35 minutes.
5. Once done, allow to release pressure naturally. Remove lid.
6. Stir well and serve.

Nutritional Value: Calories 217; Fat 6.1g; Carbohydrates 6.2g; Protein 33.4g

Recipe 76: Lemon Chicken Skewers

Serving Size: 6

Cooking Time: 25 minutes

Ingredients:

- 3 medium - 1.5-inch slices Zucchini
- 2 cloves of garlic, minced
- 3 medium onions, cut into wedges
- 12 Cherry tomatoes
- 1 ½ lb. Chicken breasts
- ¼ cup Olive oil
- 1 tablespoon White wine vinegar
- ½ teaspoon Sugar
- 3 tablespoon Lemon juice
- 1 teaspoon Salt
- 2 teaspoon Grated lemon zest
- ¼ teaspoon Black pepper
- ¼ teaspoon Dried oregano

Directions:

1. Half the zucchini lengthwise and cut it into 1.5-inch pieces.
2. Peel the onions and cut them into wedges. Zest the lemon. Cut the chicken into 1.5-inch pieces.
3. Prepare the marinade. Combine the sugar, pepper, oregano, salt, lemon zest, vinegar, lemon juice, and oil. Reserve ¼ cup for basting. Fold in the chicken and toss to cover.
4. Add the rest of the marinade in a mixing container with the tomatoes, onions, and zucchini. Put a top or layer of plastic film/foil over the dish and store in the refrigerator overnight (for best results) or a minimum of four hours.
5. When ready to cook, drain, and trash the marinade. Soak the wooden skewers in water.
6. Thread the chicken and veggies onto the wet skewers.
7. Arrange the skewers on the grill for six minutes using the medium heat setting. It's done when poked with a fork - the juices will run clear.

Nutritional Value: Calories 219; Fat 6g; Carbohydrates 17g; Protein 29g

Recipe 77: Lemon Rainbow Trout

Serving Size: 2

Cooking Time: 15 minutes

Ingredients:

- 2 rainbow trout
- Juice of 1 lemon
- 3 tablespoons olive oil
- 4 garlic cloves, minced
- A pinch of salt and black pepper

Directions:

1. Line a prepared baking sheet with parchment paper, add the fish and the rest of the ingredients and rub.
2. Bake at 400 degrees F for 15 minutes, divide between plates and serve with a side salad.

Nutritional Value: Calories 521; Fat 29g; Carbohydrates 14g; Protein 52g

Recipe 78: Lemon Salmon with Basil

Serving Size: 4

Cooking Time: 10 minutes

Ingredients:

- 4 6-ounces salmon fillet, frozen, thawed
- 2 tablespoons sliced basil, fresh, divided
- 2 medium lemons, sliced
- ¼ teaspoon ground black pepper
- ½ teaspoon salt
- 2 tablespoons olive oil
- 1 tablespoon grated lemon zest

Directions:

1. Switch on the oven. set the temperature to 375 degrees F, or 190 degrees C, and let it preheat.
2. Meanwhile, take a 15 by 10-inch baking pan, and spray it with cooking spray to grease it.
3. Then place the salmon into the prepared baking pan, drizzle oil on top, and sprinkle salt all around.
4. Sprinkle lemon zest, basil, and black pepper, place the lemon slices on top of the salmon and bake for 20 minutes, or until soft, and flakey.
5. When done, place the prepared salmon on a serving plate, sprinkle basil on top, and serve.

Nutritional Value: Calories 294; Fat 18g; Carbohydrates 3g; Protein 29g

Recipe 79: Roasted Acorn Squash with Sage

Serving Size: 4

Cooking Time: 35 minutes

Ingredients:

- 1/8 cup chopped sage leaves
- 1 1/3 tablespoons fresh thyme leaves
- 1 1/3 acorn squash, medium to large
- 1 1/3 tablespoons extra-virgin olive oil
- 2/3 teaspoon salt, plus more for seasoning
- 3 1/3 tablespoons unsalted butter (optional)
- 1/3 teaspoon freshly ground black pepper

Directions:

1. Preheat the oven to a heat of 400 degrees Fahrenheit/200 degrees Celsius/Fan 180 degrees Celsius. An acorn squash should be cut in half lengthwise. Scrape the seeds using a spoon and cut them into 14-inch thick slices horizontally.
2. Season the squash with the olive oil, sprinkle with salt, and toss to coat in a large mixing basin.
3. Place the acorn squash on a baking pan and set aside.
4. Cook the squash in the pan for 20 minutes in the oven. Cook for another 15 minutes after flipping the pumpkin with a spatula.
5. In a large-sized saucepan over medium heat, melt the butter (if using).
6. In the heated butter, cook the sage and thyme for 30 seconds.
7. Put the cooked pumpkin slices on a platter. Pour the herb butter mixture over the pumpkin. Season with prepared salt and black pepper to taste. Serve immediately.
8. Enjoy!

Nutritional Value: Calories 188; Fat 15g; Carbohydrates 16g; Protein 1g

Recipe 80: Rosemary Baked Chicken Drumsticks

Serving Size: 6

Cooking Time: 1 hour

Ingredients:

- 2 tablespoons chopped fresh rosemary leaves
- 1 teaspoon garlic powder
- ½ teaspoon sea salt
- 1/8 teaspoon freshly ground black pepper
- Zest of 1 lemon
- 12 chicken drumsticks

Directions:

1. Preheat the oven to 350°F.
2. Blend rosemary, garlic powder, sea salt, pepper, and lemon zest.
3. Situate drumsticks in a 9-by-13-inch baking dish and sprinkle with the rosemary mixture. Bake for about 1 hour.

Nutritional Value: Calories 263; Fat 6g; Carbohydrates 46g; Protein 26g

Recipe 81: Rosemary Creamy Beef

Serving Size: 4

Cooking Time: 40 minutes

Ingredients:

- 2 lbs beef stew meat, cubed
- 2 tablespoon fresh parsley, chopped
- 1 teaspoon garlic, minced
- 1/2 teaspoon dried rosemary
- 1 teaspoon chili powder
- 1 cup beef stock
- 1 cup heavy cream
- 1 onion, chopped
- 1 tablespoon olive oil
- Pepper
- Salt

Directions:

1. Add oil into the instant pot and set the pot on sauté mode.
2. Add rosemary, garlic, onion, and chili powder and sauté for 5 minutes.
3. Add meat and cook for 5 minutes.
4. Add remaining ingredients and stir well.
5. Seal pot with lid and cook on high for 30 minutes.
6. Once done, allow to eventually release pressure naturally for 10 minutes then release remaining using quick release. Remove lid.
7. Serve and enjoy.

Nutritional Value: Calories 574; Fat 29g; Carbohydrates 4.3g; Protein 70.6g

Recipe 82: Salsa Fish Fillets

Serving Size: 4

Cooking Time: 5 minutes

Ingredients:

- 1 lb tilapia fillets
- 1/2 cup salsa
- 1 cup of water
- Pepper
- Salt

Directions:

1. Place fish fillets on aluminum foil and top with salsa and season with pepper and salt.
2. Fold foil around the fish fillets.
3. Pour water into the instant pot and place trivet in the pot.
4. Place foil fish packet on the trivet.
5. Seal pot with lid and cook on high for 2 minutes.
6. Once done, release pressure using quick release. Remove lid.
7. Serve and enjoy.

Nutritional Value: Calories 342; Fat 10.5g; Carbohydrates 41.5g; Protein 18.9g

Recipe 83: Seafood Stew

Serving Size: 6

Cooking Time: 30 minutes

Ingredients:

- 1 tablespoon oil
- garlic cloves, minced
- 1 teaspoon kosher salt
- 1 cup dry white wine
- 1 large onion, diced
- 1 bay leaf
- 1 28-ounce can dice tomatoes
- 1/2-pound clams
- 1/2-pound shrimp, peeled and deveined
- 1/2-pound shrimp, peeled and deveined
- 1 cup clam juice
- 1/2-pound mussels
- 1/4 cup of minced parsley, for garnish, optional

Directions:

1. Take a large pot, heat oil by using medium heat.
2. Put the onions and cook for 3-4 minutes, until tender. Add garlic and sauté for another minute.
3. Combine the wine, tomatoes, clam juice, bay leaf, and salt in a mixing bowl. Bring to a boil, then reduce to a simmer for 20 minutes.
4. Add all of the seafood at the same time and whisk to mix. Cook for 5-7 minutes, until shrimp, is pink and cooked through, and mussels and clams open.
5. Finely, Garnish with parsley if desired and serve immediately

Nutritional Value: Calories 234; Fat 7g; Carbohydrates 26g; Protein 56g

Recipe 84: Shrimp Zoodles

Serving Size: 2

Cooking Time: 10 minutes

Ingredients:

- 2 zucchini, spiralized
- 1 lb shrimp, peeled and deveined
- 1/2 teaspoon paprika
- 1 tablespoon basil, chopped
- 1/2 lemon juice
- 1 teaspoon garlic, minced
- 2 tablespoon olive oil
- 1 cup vegetable stock
- Pepper
- Salt

Directions:

1. Add oil into the inner pot of instant pot and set the pot on sauté mode.
2. Add garlic and sauté for a minute.
3. Add shrimp and lemon juice and stir well and cook for 1 minute.
4. Add remaining ingredients and stir well.
5. Seal pot with lid and cook on high for 3 minutes.
6. Once done, release pressure using quick release. Remove lid.
7. Serve and enjoy.

Nutritional Value: Calories 215; Fat 9.2g; Carbohydrates 5.8g; Protein 27.3g

Recipe 85: Smoked Pork Sausage

Serving Size: 4

Cooking Time: 15 minutes

Ingredients:

- 1/2-pound smoked pork sausage, ground
- 2/3 teaspoon ginger-garlic paste
- 1 1/3 tablespoons scallions, minced
- 2/3 tablespoon butter, room temperature
- 2/3 tomato, pureed
- 2 2/3 ounces mozzarella cheese, crumbled
- 1 1/3 tablespoons flaxseed meal
- 5 1/3 ounces cream cheese, room temperature
- Sea salt and ground black pepper, to taste

Directions:

1. In a frying pan over medium-high heat, melt the butter. Cook for approximately 4 minutes, disintegrating the sausage with a spatula. Cook for 6 minutes over medium-low heat after adding the ginger-garlic paste, scallions, and tomato. Mix in the rest of the shopping list.
2. Refrigerate the mixture for 1 to 2 hours, or until firm. Roll the mixture into little balls.
3. Storing
4. Transfer the balls to airtight containers and store them in the fridge for up to 3 days.
5. Freeze in a prepared freezer-safe container for up to 1 month.
6. Enjoy!

Nutritional Value: Calories 386; Fat 32g; Carbohydrates 5.1g; Protein 16.7g

Recipe 86: Swordfish with Orange

Serving Size: 4

Cooking Time: 20 minutes

Ingredients:

- 4 slices of swordfish (about 21 oz)
- 1 orange
- 1.4 oz extra virgin olive oil + 1 tablespoon
- 4 tablespoons of white wine
- 1 clove of garlic
- 3 sprigs of basil
- 1 pinch of oregano
- 1 pinch of salt
- 1 pinch of pepper

Directions:

1. Preheat the oven to 356°F. Grate the prepared orange zest and squeeze out the juice. Chop the garlic and basil.
2. Heat the oil in a large-sized pot and then add the chopped garlic and basil, grated orange zest, oregano, 3 tablespoons orange juice, wine, salt and pepper and cook for 5 minutes.
3. Brush an ovenproof dish with a tablespoon of oil, then arrange the cod slices. Drizzle with the sauce and place in the oven. Bake for 20 minutes. Serve hot.

Nutritional Value: Calories 312; Fat 20.1g; Carbohydrates 2.9g; Protein 30.1g

Recipe 87: Tender Chicken Quesadilla

Serving Size: 4

Cooking Time: 20 minutes

Ingredients:

- 2 bread tortillas
- 1 teaspoon butter
- 2 teaspoon olive oil
- 1 teaspoon Taco seasoning
- 6 oz chicken breast, skinless, boneless, sliced
- 1/3 cup Cheddar cheese, shredded
- 1 bell pepper, cut on the wedges

Directions:

1. Pour 1 teaspoon of olive oil in the large-sized skillet and add chicken.
2. Sprinkle the meat with Taco seasoning and mix up well.
3. Roast chicken for 10 minutes over the medium heat. Stir it from time to time.
4. Then transfer the cooked chicken in the plate.
5. Add remaining olive oil in the skillet.
6. Then add bell pepper and roast it for 5 minutes. Stir it all the time.
7. Mix up together bell pepper with chicken.
8. Toss butter in the skillet and melt it.
9. Put 1 tortilla in the skillet.
10. Put Cheddar cheese on the tortilla and flatten it.
11. Then add chicken-pepper mixture and cover it with the second tortilla.
12. Roast the quesadilla for 2 minutes from each side.
13. Cut the cooked meal on the halves and transfer in the serving plates.

Nutritional Value: Calories 167; Fat 8.2g; Carbohydrates 16.4g; Protein 24.2g

Recipe 88: Tilapia Fillet with Onion and Avocado

Serving Size: 6

Cooking Time: 10 minutes

Ingredients:

- 1 1/2 tablespoon freshly squeezed orange juice
- 6 (4-ounce/113-g) tilapia fillets, more oblong than square, skin-on or skinned
- 1/3 cup chopped red onion
- 1 1/2 tablespoon extra-virgin olive oil
- 1/3 teaspoon kosher or sea salt
- 1 1/2 avocado, pitted, skinned, and sliced

Directions:

1. Using a fork, combine the oil, orange juice, and salt in a 9-inch glass cake pan. Working with one fillet at a time, set it in the pan and flipped it to cover it on both sides. Arrange the fillets in a wagon wheel pattern, with one end of each fillet in the center of the plate and the other end draped over the plate's edge. 1 tablespoon of onion on each fillet, then fold the end of the fillet that hangs from the edge above the onion in half.
2. When done, you should have four folded fillets, with the crease against the plate's outer edge and the ends all in the center. Cover the dish with cling film, leaving a tiny gap around the edge to allow steam to escape. microwaving for 3 minutes on high. When gently prodded with a fork, the fish begins to split into flakes (parts). Serve the fillets with the avocado as a garnish.
3. When ready, serve.

Nutritional Value: Calories 210; Fat 10g; Carbohydrates 5g; Protein 25g

Recipe 89: Turkey Curry

Serving Size: 3

Cooking Time: 40 minutes

Ingredients:

- 450g (1lb), turkey breasts, chopped
- 100g (3½ oz.) fresh rocket (arugula) leaves
- cloves garlic, chopped
- teaspoon medium curry powder
- teaspoon turmeric powder
- tablespoon fresh coriander (cilantro), finely chopped
- bird's eye chilies, chopped
- red onions, chopped
- 400ml (14fl oz.) full-fat coconut milk
- 1 tablespoon of olive oil

Directions:

1. Cook the red onions in the olive oil for 5 minutes until tender.
2. Stir in the garlic and the turkey and cook it for 7-8 minutes.
3. Stir in the turmeric, chilies, and curry powder, then add the coconut milk and coriander cilantro).
4. Bring to a boil, then reduce to a simmer for 10 minutes.
5. Scatter the rocket (arugula) onto plates and spoon the curry on top.
6. Serve alongside brown rice.

Nutritional Value: Calories 400; Fat 6g; Carbohydrates 3g; Protein 14g

Recipe 90: White Bean and Kale Soup with Chicken

Serving Size: 6

Cooking Time: 30 minutes

Ingredients:

- Sea salt + black pepper
- 3 cups kale
- 1 15-oz can white beans
- 2 cups chicken
- 1 strip bacon
- 4 cloves garlic
- 8 cups broth
- 1 cup white onion
- 1 tablespoon avocado oil

Directions:

1. Over moderate flame, heat a large pan or casserole dish. Once the pan is warmed, add the bacon or oil. Allow for two minutes of cooking time, stirring occasionally.
2. Cook, stirring periodically, for 4-5 minutes, or until onions becomes transparent and citrusy.
3. Then add garlic and cook for another 2-3 minutes. Carry to a boil the broth, completely soaked white beans and meat.
4. To blend the flavors, cook for ten minutes. After that, sprinkle with salt and pepper. Insert the kale over the last few minutes before serving. Serve instantly.

Nutritional Value: Calories 280; Fat 12.1g; Carbohydrates 7.4g; Protein 34g

Chapter 4:   Dessert Recipes

Recipe 91: Blueberry and Oats Crisp

Serving Size: 8

Cooking Time: 15 minutes

Ingredients:

- 1 cup rolled oats
- ½ cup whole wheat flour
- ¼ cup extra-virgin olive oil
- ¼ teaspoon salt
- 1 teaspoon cinnamon
- ⅓ cup honey
- Cooking oil
- 4 cups blueberries (thawed if frozen)

Directions:

1. Combine the rolled oats, flour, olive oil, salt, cinnamon, and honey in a large bowl.
2. Spray a barrel pan with cooking oil all over the bottom and sides of the pan.
3. Spread the blueberries on the bottom of the barrel pan. Top with the oat mixture.
4. Place the pan in the air fryer. Cook at 350°F (177°C) for 15 minutes.
5. Cool before serving.

Nutritional Value: Calories 304; Fat 18.9g; Carbohydrates 23.8g; Protein 10g

Recipe 92: Cherry Clafoutis

Serving Size: 6

Cooking Time: 1 hour

Ingredients:

- 1 ¼ pounds of sweet cherries
- 3 large eggs
- ½ cup of all-purpose flour
- 1 teaspoon of vanilla extract
- 1/8 teaspoon of almond extract
- ½ cup and 3 tablespoons of sugar
- 1 ⅓ cup of whole milk
- Softened butter, for the baking dish

Directions:

1. Preheat your oven at 375°F. Grease a 2 quarts of baking dish with butter. Spread the pitted cherries onto the baking dish.
2. Blend the eggs with the flour, vanilla and the rest of the ingredients in a blender until smooth. Pour this mixed mixture into the baking dish and bake for 45 minutes. Serve.

Nutritional Value: Calories 352; Fat 15g; Carbohydrates 51g; Protein 34g

Recipe 93: Cinnamon Stuffed Peaches

Serving Size: 4

Cooking Time: 15 minutes

Ingredients:

- 4 peaches, pitted, halved
- 2 tablespoons ricotta cheese
- 2 tablespoons of liquid honey
- ¾ cup of water
- ½ teaspoon vanilla extract
- ¾ teaspoon ground cinnamon
- 1 tablespoon of almonds, sliced
- ¾ teaspoon saffron

Directions:

1. Pour water in the saucepan and bring to boil.
2. Add vanilla extract, saffron, ground cinnamon, and liquid honey.
3. Cook the liquid until the honey is melted.
4. Then remove it from the heat.
5. Put the halved peaches in the hot honey liquid.
6. Meanwhile, make the filling: mix up together ricotta cheese, vanilla extract, and sliced almonds.
7. Remove the peaches from the honey liquid and arrange them on the plate. Fill 4 peach halves with ricotta filling and cover them with remaining peach halves.
8. Sprinkle the cooked dessert with liquid honey mixture gently.

Nutritional Value: Calories 213; Fat 1.4g; Carbohydrates 23.9g; Protein 1.9g

Recipe 94: Citrus Ciambella

Serving Size: 10

Cooking Time: 35 minutes

Ingredients:

- 1 ½ cups granulated sugar
- 1 tablespoon lemon zest
- ½ cup lemon juice
- 5 large eggs
- ½ cup light-tasting olive oil
- 2 cups all-purpose flour
- 2 teaspoons baking powder
- ½ teaspoon salt
- Confectioners' sugar (optional)
- Nonstick cooking spray

Directions:

1. Preheat the oven to 350°F. Spray a Bundt pan with cooking spray.
2. In a mixing bowl, mix the sugar, eggs and zest. Whisk well.
3. Mix in the lemon juice and oil.
4. Add the flour, baking powder and salt. Combine well.
5. Pour the already prepared batter into the prepared pan and bake for 35–40 minutes until a toothpick inserted comes out clean.
6. Dust with confectioners' sugar (if using).

Nutritional Value: Calories 264; Fat 15g; Carbohydrates 30g; Protein 2g

Recipe 95: Fruit Crumble Mug Cakes

Serving Size: 4

Cooking Time: 20 minutes

Ingredients:

- 1 small peach, cored, diced
- 4 plums, pitted, diced
- 2 tablespoons oats
- 1 small apple, cored, diced
- 4 ounces almond flour
- 1 small pear, diced
- 2 tablespoons swerve caster sugar
- 1 ¾ tablespoon coconut sugar
- 1 tablespoon honey
- 2 ounces unsalted butter
- ¼ cup blueberries, diced

Directions:

1. Switch on the air fryer, insert fryer basket, grease it with olive oil, then shut with its lid, set the fryer at 320 degrees F, and preheat for 5 minutes.
2. Meanwhile, take four heatproof mugs or ramekins, evenly fill them with fruits, and then cover with coconut sugar and honey.
3. Place flour in a bowl, add butter and caster sugar, rub with fingers until the mixture resembles crumbs, stir in oats, and evenly spoon this mixture into prepared fruit mugs.
4. Open the fryer, place fruit mugs in it, close with its lid, cook for 10 minutes, then increase air fryer temperature to 390 degrees F and continue cooking for 5 minutes until the top have nicely browned and crunchy.
5. When the air fryer beeps, open its lid, carefully take out the mugs and serve straight away.

Nutritional Value: Calories 380; Fat 11g; Carbohydrates 68g; Protein 5g

Recipe 96: Rhubarb Strawberry Crunch

Serving Size: 8

Cooking Time: 40 minutes

Ingredients:

- 1 cup of white sugar
- 3 tablespoons of all-purpose flour
- 3 cups of fresh strawberries, sliced
- 3 cups of rhubarb, cut into cubes
- 1 ½ cups of flour
- 1 cup of packed brown sugar
- 1 cup of butter
- 1 cup of oatmeal

Directions:

1. Preheat the oven to 190 ° C. Incorporate white sugar, 3 tablespoons flour, strawberries and rhubarb in a large bowl. Place the prepared mixture in a 9 x 13-inch baking dish.
2. Mix 1 ½ cups of flour, brown sugar, butter, and oats until a crumbly texture is obtained. You may want to use a blender for this. Crumble the mixture of rhubarb and strawberry. Bake for 45 minutes.

Nutritional Value: Calories 253; Fat 10.8g; Carbohydrates 32g; Protein 2.3g

Recipe 97: Rose Crème Caramel

Serving Size: 2

Cooking Time: 35 minutes

Ingredients:

- 2 eggs
- 1 cup of low fat cream
- 1 cup of milk
- 2 tablespoons of sugar
- 1 tablespoon of rose syrup
- Caramel syrup
- 2 tablespoons of sugar
- 2 tablespoons of water

Directions:

1. Mix the tablespoons of water and sugar in a saucepan and cook until it caramelizes, stirring occasionally. Divide the caramel into 4 ramekins. Preheat your oven at 350°F.
2. In a bowl, beat the eggs with rose syrup, sugar, cream and milk. Divide this mixture into the ramekins then bake for 25 minutes. Allow the crème caramel to cool then refrigerate for 6 hours. Run a knife around the dessert and flip onto a serving plate. Serve.

Nutritional Value: Calories 358; Fat 20.8g; Carbohydrates 31.9g; Protein 13.1g

Recipe 98: Vanilla Bread Pudding with Apricots

Serving Size: 6

Cooking Time: 15 minutes

Ingredients:

- 2 tablespoons coconut oil
- 1 1/3 cups heavy cream
- 4 eggs, whisked
- 1/2 cup dried apricots, soaked and chopped
- 1 teaspoon cinnamon, ground
- 1/2 teaspoon star anise, ground
- A pinch of grated nutmeg
- A pinch of salt
- 1/2 cup granulated sugar
- 2 tablespoons molasses
- 2 cups milk
- 4 cups Italian bread, cubed
- 1 teaspoon vanilla paste

Directions:

1. Add 1 ½ cups of water and a metal rack to the Instant Pot.
2. Grease a baking dish with a nonstick cooking spray. Throw the bread cubes into the prepared baking dish.
3. In a mixing bowl, thoroughly combine the remaining ingredients. Pour the mixture over the bread cubes. Cover with a piece of foil, making a foil sling.
4. Secure the lid. Choose the "Porridge" mode and High pressure; cook for 15 minutes. Once cooking is complete, use a quick pressure release; carefully remove the lid. Enjoy!

Nutritional Value: Calories 410; Fat 24.3g; Carbohydrates 37.4g; Protein 11.5g

Recipe 99: White Chocolate Brie Cups

Serving Size: 15

Cooking Time: 25 minutes

Ingredients:

- 1/3 cup orange marmalade
- Kumquat slices
- 1 ounce's white chocolate
- 2 ounces Brie cheese
- 1 package phyllo tart shells

Directions:

1. Preheat the oven to 350 degrees Fahrenheit. Fill each tart casing halfway with chocolate, then halfway with cheddar.
2. Place on a cookie dish that hasn't been buttered. Serve with a dollop of marmalade on top.
3. Preheat oven to 375°F and bake for 6-8 minutes, or until lightly browned.
4. Warm the dish before serving. Kumquats may be added on the top if desired.

Nutritional Value: Calories 236; Fat 2g; Carbohydrates 17.4g; Protein 4.5g

Recipe 100:   Wine Figs

Serving Size: 2

Cooking Time: 8 minutes

Ingredients:

- 1/2 cup of pine nuts
- 1 cup of red wine
- 1 pound of figs
- Sugar, as needed

Directions:

1. Slowly pour the wine and sugar into the Instant Pot. Arrange the trivet inside it; place the figs over it. Close the lid and lock. Ensure that you have sealed the valve to avoid leakage.
2. Press MANUAL mode and set timer to 3 minutes. After the timer reads zero, press CANCEL and quick-release pressure. Carefully remove the lid. Divide figs into bowls, and drizzle wine from the pot over them. Top with pine nuts and enjoy.

Nutritional Value: Calories 95; Fat 3g; Carbohydrates 5g; Protein 2g

Chapter 5:   28-Day Meal Plan

Day	Breakfast	Lunch	Dinner
1	Parmesan Ham Frittata	Sailor Clams	Chicken Marsala
2	Greek Breakfast Bagel	Artichoke Beef Roast	Greek Lamb Chop
3	Stuffed Pita Breads	Chicken and Mint Sauce	Shrimp Zoodles
4	Raspberry Oats	Sage Tomato Beef	Eggplant Ratatouille
5	Creamy Parsley Souffle	Dijon Fish Fillets	Salsa Fish Fillets
6	Zucchini Oats	Cayenne Cod and Tomatoes	Italian Shredded Pork Stew
7	Nectarine Bruschetta	Asparagus Risotto	Ground Pork Skillet
8	Mediterranean Frittata	Shrimp Lunch Rolls	Baked Falafel
9	Tomato and Spinach Egg Wraps	Baked Salmon with Garlic Cilantro Sauce	Roasted Acorn Squash with Sage
10	Artichoke Frittata	Swordfish Pizzaiola	Chicken Stroganoff
11	Hummus Deviled Egg	Pesto Fish Fillet	Swordfish with Orange
12	Mediterranean Omelet	Carrot Mushrom Beef Roast	Jalapeno Beef Chili
13	Bacon and Brie Omelet Wedges	White Pizza with Broccoli Crust	Fish Stew with Tomatoes and Olives
14	Baked Pasta	Mushroom Cream Turkey	Turkey Curry
15	Avocado Baked Eggs	Chicken Kebabs	Lemon Chicken Skewers
16	Buttery Pancakes	Asparagus Risotto	Smoked Pork Sausage
17	Lean and Green Chicken Pesto Pasta	Pan-Seared Trout with Tzatziki	White Bean and Kale Soup with Chicken
18	Quinoa Muffins	Lamb and Potatoes Stew	Garlicky Clams
19	Baked Pasta	Scallions and Salmon Tartar	Lemon Salmon with Basil

20	Rice Stuffed Tomatoes	Broiled Salmon	Cabbage Roll Casserole with Veal
21	Tuna Breakfast Quiche	Seafood Gumbo	Bked Falafel
22	Heavenly Egg Bake with Blackberry	Herb and Pistachio Turkey Breasts	Tilapia Fillet with Onion and Avocado
23	Mushroom and Zucchini Egg Muffins	White Pizza with Broccoli Crust	Rosemary Baked Chicken Drumsticks
24	Cheesy Green Bites	Herbed Almond Turkey	Baked Oysters with Tasso Cream
25	Quinoa Muffins	Oyster Stew	Lemon Rainbow Trout
26	Fig and Ricotta Overnight Oats	Thyme Ginger Garlic Beef	Chicken with Tomato-Balsamic Pan Sauce
27	Poached Eggs with Avocado Puree	Salmon and Creamy Endives	Fish Stew with Tomatoes and Olives
28	Cheesy Eggs in Avocado	Grilled Lemon Chiken	Tender Chicken Quesadilla

8. Conclusion

If you actually have an interest in losing weight and improving your health, try adding into your diet the components of the Mediterranean diet.

You may not be able to go cold turkey because some foods are so ingrained in our culture that it will take some getting used to. In fact, many people will start to notice their health and wellbeing immeasurably improve after only a few weeks on this diet. You may even be able to lose as much as ten or fifteen pounds in one month's time! It's true that this diet is very low in calories and is not a typical weight loss plan. You must be disciplined to carry it out, but you'll be glad you did.

This healthy eating plan has proven to be an excellent resource for fighting heart disease, lowering blood pressure, reducing cholesterol levels and improving concentration and memory. It can help you either lose weight or maintain a healthy weight if you are sick of trying all the other fad diets.

The Mediterranean diet has been linked to some of the strongest health benefits available today - even more so when combined with a daily workout routine. As always, it's important to pay attention to your body and your own unique health needs when making changes in your diet or lifestyle. You should actually also consult your physician before beginning any new diet or exercise regimen.

Remember, the Mediterranean diet is not just about food; it also gives you some great nutritional ideas for how to always stay healthy. When you're healthy, nothing else really matters. You will never have to deal with disease, and you can maintain your quality of life as you get older.

So, go ahead and give the Mediterranean diet a try and enjoy a lifetime of great health!

9. Index

Printed in Great Britain
by Amazon

13460104R00066